THE WOKE INVERSION

How Intersectional Theory Ruined Everything

Written by Mark Fairley

MORE TITLES FROM THE FUEL PROJECT

Trench
A Christian Guide to the Culture War

Stay Free
Why Society Can't Survive Without God

The War On Truth
How A Generation Abandoned Reality

The Restless Church
Rediscovering New Testament Christianity

The Coming Summer
Exploring The Signs of Jesus' Return

The Secret of Joy
Ten Biblical Antidotes for Depression & Anxiety

Revelation
The Fuel Project Guide

The Reason For Pain
Why God Allows Suffering

thefuelproject.org

Visit our website for a complete list of books and video series.

"What sorrow for those who say
that evil is good and good is evil,
that dark is light and light is dark,
that bitter is sweet and sweet is bitter."

Isaiah 5:20

CONTENTS

Introduction

GENERALITIES

1. Hatred
2. The Male Privilege Myth
3. The White Privilege Myth
4. Inverting Status
5. The Victimhood Olympics
6. The Benefits of Victimhood
7. Enfeebled
8. Division
9. Paranoia
10. Uncharitable
11. Turning Good Into Evil

SPECIFICS

12. What Men Do
13. What Women Do
14. Marriage Benefits Adults
15. Marriage Benefits Kids
16. Homosexuality
17. Transgenderism
18. Contagion
19. Christianity
20. Other Faiths aka Islam
21. The West
22. Obesity

Conclusion

INTRODUCTION

(A quick recap of "Trench")

In the book before this one—called ***"Trench"***—I set out to establish a Christian perspective on the culture war that has engulfed the world in the early decades of the 21st Century.

In that volume, we built a foundational understanding of why the world has come to be so divided into political Lefts and Rights, and I explained the key to understanding both sides. The Left (or Liberals) are primarily driven by "The Soft Virtues" which emanate from the heart and are made up of things like Love, Grace, Mercy, Compassion and Kindness. The Right (Conservatives) are primarily driven "The Hard Virtues" which emanate from the head and contains things like Truth, Justice, Righteousness and Reason. This is a partial reproduction of the graphic we concluded with in that book & subsequent video series.

SOFT VIRTUES	HARD VIRTUES
(Liberal Priorities)	(Conservative Priorities)
Love	Truth
Mercy	Justice
Grace	Righteousness
Compassion	Lawfulness
Forgiveness	Fairness
Peace	Competition
Equality	Reason
Unity	Individual Freedom
Safety	Risk

Both the virtue sets are fundamentally good. Who can argue that love and mercy is bad? Or truth and justice for that matter? What may not immediately be obvious however—and this is something we covered in depth through *"Trench"*—is that these two value sets are often in conflict.

The example I used to illustrate the problem was of a guilty criminal who had been arrested and placed on trial. If the judge presiding over the case was to prioritise Soft Love, Compassion and Mercy, he would let the man walk free to give him a second chance in life. If the judge prioritised Hard Truth, Righteousness and Justice however, he would sentence him to prison to pay for his crimes. Herein lies the problem. Love and Mercy are good and they say, "set him free." Yet Truth and Justice are equally good and they say, "lock him up." Which set do you prioritise then? Which ones are more important?

This conflict of goods is the fundamental reason why neither Liberals or Conservatives, despite centuries of debate, have ever fully managed to win the argument. It's not that one side is motivated by evil and the other is motivated by good. It's more accurate to say that that

Liberals and Conservatives both believe in good, but they believe in different *kinds* of good. Conflicting kinds of good.

The conflict plays out in real-life circumstances and in the debate around current events every day. For example, in recent years, illegal immigration has become a major problem for Western nations as millions of people from different cultures flock towards them in search of a better life. Finding that legal routes are often limited, they instead pay traffickers to help them break through national borders illicitly. Equipped with knowledge of *"The Trench Theory,"* the response of the Left and Right around this issue has been entirely predictable. The Left, primarily driven by Soft Compassion, think, "these poor, hungry souls must be so desperate. We must let them all in and give them free food and shelter. They may be entering illegally but that merely highlights their desperation and is all the more reason to help!" The Right, on the other hand, prioritising Hard Truth and Justice, ask questions. "Are all these people really refugees or simply economic migrants? We should test for this. Can our infrastructure and public finances support such a massive influx? Surely the criminality of traffickers should never be rewarded. Send them back so that others aren't encouraged to follow them and thus exacerbate the issue." And so, although both Liberals and Conservatives are being driven by essentially good values, the two political factions are now in conflict about the proper outcome. The Left wants to let everyone in and the Right wants to send them back.

The Balance

Although we can say that both sides are driven by kinds of good, there is however the threat of extremism. Extremism happens when one side becomes so contemptuous of the opposing virtue set, that they reject it entirely. In doing so, they fall into evil. For example, the Far Right may reject love and compassion so completely that they come to view other people as inferior or even sub-human. Likewise, the Far Left may reject truth and reason so absolutely that they begin hating it and anyone who tries to speak it—curbing free-speech and moving towards a kind of collectivist totalitarianism. This of course, is exactly what we see in Far Left societies like North Korea. There are many more problems of detaching from a whole virtue sets of course, but they were discussed in *"Trench"* and we won't get into them again now.

What we ideally want then, I believe, is to hold both the virtue sets in balance. We need to somehow establish within ourselves—and consequently in the wider world—the idea that it's important to be both compassionate yet still committed to the truth; to be loving yet still committed to justice. This is the kind of attitude I believe God wants us to have and indeed, it's what we see symbolised in the cross of Jesus Christ. After all, the cross tells us that God is so just and righteous that he must punish all sin with death, yet the cross also tells us God is so loving and compassionate that he sent his one and only begotten Son into the world to take that punishment upon himself. The cross therefore becomes the place where all virtue meets and is held in balance. It is both Hard and Soft. It speaks of both judgement and mercy. We must find a way to manifest that same balance in ourselves and in our society.

The Slide Towards The Far Left

The problem for our time is that the West is currently out of balance and falling into Leftist extremism. Since a cultural revolution that took place in 1967, and which heralded the beginning of the Postmodern Age, our culture has been increasingly convinced by the notion that Soft Love, Compassion and Kindness is all we need. Conversely, our culture has increasingly begun to revile the apparently opposed virtues of Hard Truth, Justice and Righteousness. In *"Trench,"* I explained how we arrived at this point, and I'll only briefly summarise it here.

It goes something like this. In the Medieval Period, which is sometimes referred to as "The Dark Ages," Western civilisation wanted for lack of knowledge and a pervading ignorance was creating terrible social problems. Our ancestors recognised it and at first through the Renaissance, and then through the Enlightenment, humanity vowed to solve its maladies with education. From that moment, we entered into "The Age of Reason," where the primary concern was the pursuit of Truth, Knowledge, Science and Wisdom…in other words, the Hard Virtues. Those favoured by Conservatives. Humanity believed that as we acquired these things, it would make for a better world—perhaps even a utopian one.

In that pursuit, we indeed gained tremendous knowledge and the world began a process of rapid technological advancement. However, as we sought Truth, people began arguing about what it was. For example, was Capitalism the best economic system or was it Socialism? Are nations best governed as Monarchies or Republics? Truth claims, as it turns out, are divisive. And these arguments soon led to wars. Indeed, much of the technology we have today exists because people were trying to win those wars. And by the middle of the 20th Century, all this warring over truth claims were beginning to make people scared. When Adolf Hitler's Nazi Germany made the claim that fascism was the best way to order Europe, and when Winston Churchill's Britain had disagreed insisting free democracy was the truth, it had led to a World War that culminated in the dropping of an atomic bomb on Hiroshima in 1945. Although this action decisively won the argument for the Allies, the world was in that moment horrified to realise that we now had weapons so powerful, they had the potential to wipe out every living creature on earth. It seemed that our quest for knowledge wasn't creating utopia as hoped, but rather a *dystopia*. Children of the 1960s envisaged a future earth that had been scorched to oblivion by nuclear warfare.

By 1967 then, people were ready to turn their back on the Enlightenment ideals. To the Sixties generation, it seemed like Truth wasn't really the answer after all. As long as people believed in absolute truth and made it their priority, there would always be wars as people fought over their own ideas of it, and if we didn't stop the wars, we would destroy the planet. What we needed most of all, they thought, was Love.

From then on, to assure the future of our planet, Love and Compassion became the thing. A cultural revolution took place around this idea—the "Summer of Love" it was called—and from that moment, the seeds of Postmodernism were planted. In the decades that followed, people would increasingly assert that that love is all we need and that there is no such thing as absolute truth. Anyone who claims there is an absolute truth is a villain and an enemy of civilisation. No. Nothing is real. Kindness and compassion is the only thing. In short, we began creating a society that centred around the Liberal Soft Virtues and that increasingly rejected the Conservative Hard Virtues as the root of all evil.

Which brings us to the present day. Since 1967, these Leftist ideas have been gradually spreading and becoming deeply entrenched in all our institutions, media outlets, education establishments, political parties and amongst the general population of the world. Those who knew and believed in the more conservative ideas that existed before 1967 are increasingly dying off and their voices and values are becoming increasingly faint. The majority of people today are now utterly convinced that the deeper into the Soft Virtues we go, the better life will be, and that anything approximating "conservatism" or "right-wing" values are evil, and should have no place in society. Thus, we are increasingly becoming detached from Truth and Reason, and all the other values of the right. We are instead becoming subject to far-left extremism.

At the time of writing this book late in 2023, the folly of this way of thinking is very clear. After six decades of rejecting Truth and Reason, we are now living in a time of lies and absurdity. It's a world where a biological man can now put on a dress and wig, insist he's a woman, and because compassion trumps facts, we are expected to affirm his fantasies. For the same reason, if someone decides they're neither male or female, but instead "non-binary," the rest of the population is compelled to agree. If a human-being insists they're really a cat or a hippo or a frog, out of "love" society insists we mustn't contradict them. If they're unhealthily obese, we have to be "kind" and pretend it's healthy and attractive. If someone proclaims that women are physically just as strong and fast as men, or even more so, we must be "nice" and nod as if they really are. If someone proclaims that homosexuality is as natural and healthy as heterosexuality, for the same reasons, we are compelled to agree.

Truth has been completely shut down. For if anyone dares to interject it into these matters, it's become common to encounter serious societal repercussions. The least of it is the name-calling designed to silence dissent. "Bigot," "hater," or "___phobe," for example. Social media companies now deplatform people who speak truth so their voices can't be heard in online spaces. Institutions may blacklist you—recently it has come to light that banks are refusing to give accounts or financial services to people who are not falling in line. Jobs are being lost because of it. Friendships are being jettisoned. Hurting feelings with facts has now even become criminalised. Increasingly, the police are arresting people who say "hurtful" things, no matter how truthful they may be.

With so much risk attached to speak the truth, free-speech has now been chilled in a most sinister way. People now often feel compelled to say silent with their true thoughts—never really speaking their mind for fear of what they could lose—or at worst, they feel compelled to affirm things they don't really believe. The move towards the far-left hasn't created utopia either; it has merely created a different kind of dystopia; a world of tyranny. Every day, we are seeing formerly free Western nations begin to conform to a collectivist ideology that previously only existed in places like Communist China and Korea.

If that brief summary of *"Trench"* makes sense, and if it resonates with you, you're now ready to jump into this book. You may still want to put this one down and read *"Trench"* first.* After all, this is intended to be a sequel. In truth, *"The Woke Inversion"* is a little more than a sequel—what I'm writing here I originally intended to be a part of *"Trench."* I only truncated *"Trench"* when I realised how long it would be if I included these pages as well. Hence, it has now become its own volume. Either way, if you've understood this brief summary, you've understood enough to be getting on with. As long as you remember the Postmodern Age is dominated by the Soft Virtues and that has meant a rejection of the Hard Virtues, that should be enough background information to launch you into this one. I'll re-print the graphic one more time so you can familiarise yourself with it before we continue.

SOFT VIRTUES (Liberal Priorities)	HARD VIRTUES (Conservative Priorities)
Love	Truth
Mercy	Justice
Grace	Righteousness
Compassion	Lawfulness
Forgiveness	Fairness
Peace	Competition
Equality	Reason
Unity	Individual Freedom
Safety	Risk

*At the time of writing, "Trench" is available in book form—paperback and e-book—at Amazon. The video series that accompanies it is available on YouTube and Rumble. If you'd like to download the series so that you have your own personal copy, that can be done by visiting thefuelproject.org.

PART 1

THE GENERAL PROBLEM

1
HATRED

Because the Left prioritises Love and Compassion, their mission is to find the people who need these things the most—they want to identify the hurting, the downtrodden, and the marginalised so they may sympathise with them, champion their cause, and offer them support. And to this point, Christians can have no argument. The Bible, after all, is filled with verses that encourage us to do this very thing.

The problem begins however, with the framework the Left have developed to identify the oppressed. It's called "Intersectional Theory" or simply "Intersectionality" for short. It was created in 1989 by an American civil rights advocate called Kimberlé Williams Crenshaw and it's defined in Wikipedia as, "…an analytical framework for understanding how a person's various social and political identities combine to create different modes of discrimination and privilege. Intersectionality identifies multiple factors of advantage and disadvantage."[1] We can easily visualise it like this:

The Woke Inversion

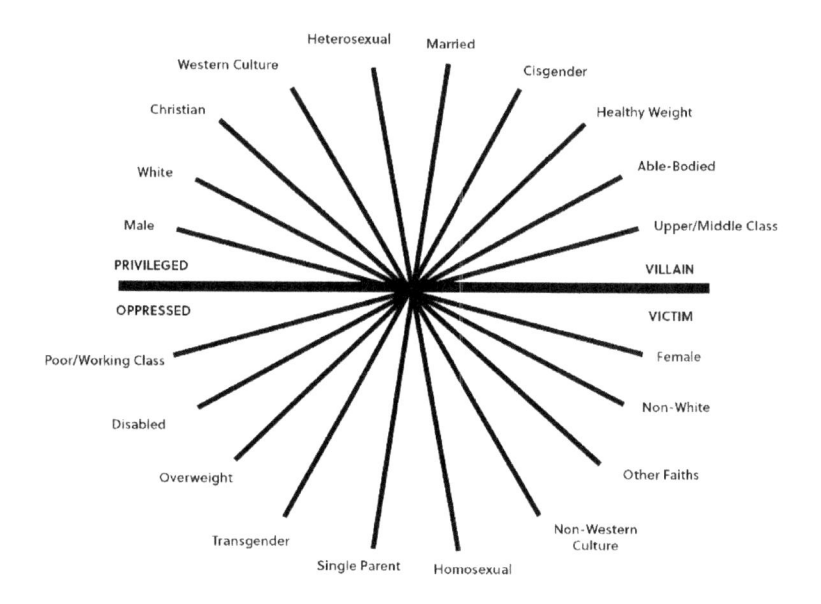

[Diagram: a radial chart with spokes labelled around a central point. Upper half labelled "PRIVILEGED" / "VILLAIN"; lower half labelled "OPPRESSED" / "VICTIM". Upper spokes (privileged): Heterosexual, Married, Western Culture, Cisgender, Christian, Healthy Weight, White, Able-Bodied, Male, Upper/Middle Class. Lower spokes (oppressed): Poor/Working Class, Female, Disabled, Non-White, Overweight, Other Faiths, Transgender, Non-Western Culture, Single Parent, Homosexual.]

According to this theory, life is best understood as a power struggle. There are some in the world who hold the power, and correspondingly those who don't. Whether an individual has power or not is deemed to depend on identity traits like Sex, Sexuality, Race, Wealth, Social Class, Religion, Country of Birth, and so forth. The more identities you can claim above the horizontal line, the more privileged with power you are considered to be (for the reason that these tend to have more physical strength, money, or are part of a majority.) The more identities you claim below the horizontal line, the more disadvantaged you are considered to be (for the converse reasons they tend to be physically weaker, poorer, or are part of a minority.)

For example, the theory says a ***man*** has one point of privilege on the basis he is physically stronger than a woman. A ***white*** man has two points of privilege on the basis his skin colour also makes him part of the majority in Western society. A white ***heterosexual*** man has three points of privilege on the basis heterosexuality is another majority orientation. Conversely, a ***woman*** is considered to have one point of disadvantage because she is physically weaker than a man; a ***black*** woman has two points of disadvantage because black skin is a minority shade in the West; and a black ***lesbian*** woman has three points of disadvantage because homosexuality is a minority orientation. The Left use this framework to identify minorities and those who they believe are most marginalised in life, and then adjust their compassion levels according to how many oppression points they think you score. The more disadvantaged you are, the more deserving of compassion, sympathy, love, praise and attention you are considered to be.

Hatred

The reverse is also true. And this is where the problems with Intersectional Theory begin. The more privilege points someone is believed to score, the more the Left will treat them with contempt. At best, the Left believe the privileged are unneedful of their compassion but at worst they believe the privileged are actually complicit in the inequality. As those who benefit most from the status quo, it's thought the powerful deliberately use their strength, money or numerical advantage to keep everyone else pinned down, treading them underfoot and profiting from their suffering. By this system's reckoning, men are natural subjugators of women; whites are natural subjugators of others races; while heterosexuals naturally marginalise homosexuals. After all, for everyone who is oppressed, there must be an oppressor. For every victim, there must be a villain. Intersectional Theory therefore characterises the privileged as life's villains and oppressors. They are the cause of the inequality in the world. Their very existence is a problem to be solved. They can do no right. They are an evil enemy. They are to be torn down and defeated. To hate the privileged, under this system, then becomes virtuous.

This brings us to the first significant problem of Intersectional Theory—it encourages hatred—and very often for the most spurious of reasons. For example, you will often find people who believe in Intersectionality spouting the most hate-filled bile against men, for no other reason than the fact they are men. In recent years, "men are trash" and "kill all men" have been trending hashtags on social media.

Likewise, people with white skin are considered evil for no other reason than the fact they have white skin. Believers in Intersectional Theory will talk openly about "abolishing whiteness" and fantasise about a future where white humans have been exterminated. Indeed, in April, 2021, a psychiatrist called Aruna Khilanani gave a speech at Yale School of Medicine called, "The Psychopathic Problem of the White Mind," in which she argued that a white person's mind is inherently and irreparably evil. In this speech, she said that she "had fantasies of unloading a revolver into the head of any white person that got in my way, burying their body and wiping my bloody hands as I walked away relatively guiltless with a bounce in my step."[2]

People who are heterosexual are treated with contempt on the basis that their existence promotes "heteronormativity"—literally just the normalness of heterosexuality. The sheer numbers of heterosexual people in the world makes it seem like the natural, ideal and coherent thing, and therefore it marginalises homosexuals and makes them feel like their minority orientation is unnatural and inferior. For this reason, believers in Intersectional Theory will talk about destroying or "completely smashing heteronormativity."[3] Elly Barnes, a lesbian woman who heads the charity, "Educate and Celebrate," has openly stated their goal is to get into British schools to transform the culture of them so that children are indoctrinated with LGBTQ ideology and come to hate heteronormativity. At LGBTQ parades, participants have also been heard chanting about trying to corrupt the next generation with their propaganda singing, "we're here, we're queer, we're coming for your children."[4]

Chanting about killing men, giving lectures about white genocide, and corrupting the innocence of children, is bad enough in itself. However, it's made worse by the fact people now hold these positions while feeling entirely convinced of their own goodness. To hate men, white people and heteronormativity is according to Intersectional Theory, a justified and noble thing. This theory tells its followers that since these are the major sources of inequality in the world—life's oppressors and villains—if people like these could just be torn down and eradicated, an egalitarian utopia would emerge.

Although they would hate to hear it, there are parallels here with the Nazis. The Nazis also rose to power declaring that there were certain troublesome groups who were holding society back and spoiling the world, and if they could just be eradicated, a utopia would emerge. For them, it was the Jews who were to blame, but is it so very different to fantasise about doing away with everyone who has *white* skin? The target of the race-hatred may be different, but it's racism nonetheless. Believers in Intersectionality would say it's impossible to be racist against white people because they're privileged and have all the power. Under their belief system, any amount of hatred against white people is warranted. Likewise, hatred for men and those who are "heteronormative." But this is exactly what makes it so dangerous—that they spout venomous hatred against whole swathes of humanity, and fantasise about killing them and dumping them in shallow graves, with the approval of their own conscience. They preach this message with a sense they are somehow on the side of good and on the right side of history. Brainwashed by Intersectional Theory, they truly believe, like the Nazis did, they would be doing humanity a favour if they could carry out their genocidal schemes. We sometimes wonder how the Nazis could have committed their hateful atrocities and convinced themselves they were on the side of good. Yet Intersectional Theory has produced a similar effect in its devotees today.

From around 2017, the people who subscribe to "Intersectional Theory" began describing themselves as "Woke." Originally, "Woke" meant being awake to the cause of the marginalised and the cries of the oppressed. Indeed, the dictionary defines it as, "being aware of and actively attentive to injustice in society, especially in regard to race, class and gender."[5] In the passing of time however, it has come to mean slightly more than that. It now generally means someone who fully subscribes to the Intersectional ideology, and who with it, harbours a burning hatred of those who they believe are life's "villains." Chiefly, straight white men. You may notice this hatred when you encounter the Woke, for it simmers only barely under the surface and is not easily contained. Indeed, you will notice that for all their talk of compassion and kindness, they are often anything but.

2
THE MALE PRIVILEGE MYTH

Perhaps the next problem worth considering with Intersectional Theory is that it's just not true. It's just not true that straight white men are inherently more privileged than anyone else in society. In many ways, it's actually the reverse. This whole framework is fundamentally flawed. Firstly, let's look at the idea men are more privileged than women.

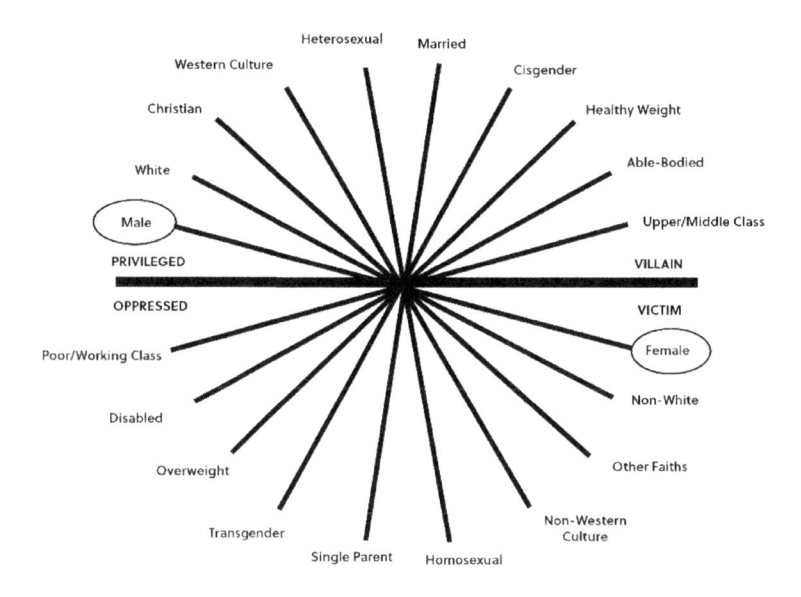

The Male Privilege Myth

In 2019, a team of scientists from the University of Essex and the University of Missouri carried out a global study across 134 different countries to determine the levels of hardship and discrimination that are present for men and women in each one. To present their findings, they compiled a database called the Basic Index of Gender Inequality (BIGI) and once all the data had been inputted, they discovered that men are more disadvantaged and face greater hardship in 91 of those countries while women are more disadvantaged and face greater hardship in 43. This means that men actually face more daily hardship in more countries than women, and this was noted to be especially true in the West. The team found that men are especially discriminated against in developed countries like the UK, USA and Australia. They pointed to the fact that in these countries and others like them, men receive greater punishments than women for the same crime, are more likely to be drafted into compulsory military service, and are far more likely to be doing dangerous and physically exhausting jobs which lead to occupational injuries and deaths.[1]

The topics the scientists raised are the tip of the iceberg. Firstly, it is true that men do receive harsher punishments than women for the same crime—something called "Sentencing Disparity." Globally, 93% of the prison population are male.[2] This is partly because men are twice as likely as women to be sentenced to jail after conviction, and on average receive 63% longer jail sentences.[3] 29% of male first-time offenders are sentenced to custody, while only 17% of female first-time offenders are.[4] Men have a 62% chance of being bailed, while women have an 80% chance. On average, men will serve 53% of their sentence, while women will serve 5% less than that.

The struggle for boys starts early in the West as it's been noted educational establishments are now primarily geared towards the advancement of girls. Psychologist Michael Thompson has noted that these days, "girl behaviour is the gold standard in schools. Boys are treated like defective girls."[5] As a result of female-centric education, across the board, boys now get lower grades than girls in school, receive fewer honours, and are far less likely to go to college. The National Assessment of Educational Progress (NAEP)—an American organisation—says that the average eighth grade girl will write at the same level as an eleventh grade boy, meaning that boys are effectively lagging three years behind.[6] For every 100 girls aged 6-14 who have difficulty with their regular schoolwork, 176 boys will have difficulty. Boys earn 70% of the "D's" and "F's" in school exams. They only earn 40% of the "A's." Boys are 50% more likely than girls to be held back a grade, are over twice as likely to be suspended, and nearly three times as likely to be expelled. Of high school dropouts, 80% are males. The ratio of non-achieving males to females is around 8 to 1. Boys are 95% more likely to be diagnosed as hyperactive and therefore boys are 70% more likely to be medicated at school age. These troubles through school mean that just 41% of US college students are now male, and for every 100 women that graduate college, only 74 men will.

The early disadvantages in school have knock-on implications as men advance through life. According to the housing charity, Crisis, 84% of the hidden homeless population in the UK are male.[4] Furthermore, 9 out of 10 of people sleeping rough are male. If men are on the streets because their home has become unsafe, according to Mankind Initiative, there are far less places compared to women where they can go to receive some kind of support. There are 33 safe houses or refuges for men in the UK if they encounter these problems, whereas there are 4,000 for women. Some may say this is because women are overwhelmingly more likely to feel unsafe at home and need somewhere else to go—women after all, are more likely to be the victims of domestic abuse. However, according to statistics gathered by

The Guardian newspaper, this isn't always true. They write, "The home has long been the focus of feminist analysis as a realm in which men are able to exert their power over women. That may be true, but the statistics on domestic abuse in marriages may well challenge your assumptions. 3.4% of married women reported a case of domestic abuse over the past year. The proportion of men? 3.4%."[4]

Should husbands and wives get divorced, men are massively disadvantaged compared to women. In the United States, women will win child custody rights 90% of the time.[7] This means that fathers are sometimes completely cut off from their children. Who gets to keep the house after a divorce is closely linked to child custody, meaning courts typically award it to the woman as well.[8] Very often, she will be granted some kind of monthly maintenance payment from the man too meaning that after divorce, he will be forced to continue funding her life. Therefore, according to a key study by the University of Amsterdam, divorce tends to impact men much harder than women in general. Men will generally experience greater health declines and report lower feelings of well-being afterwards.[9] They will be at higher risk of adopting bad coping habits like alcohol or drugs, they will have an elevated mortality risk, they will experience a disproportionate decline in family life satisfaction, they will experience higher dissatisfaction with custodial arrangements, and they will report greater feelings of loneliness and social isolation. This makes marriage an especially risky endeavour for a man, who may very well face complete ruin should it not work out. It's especially dangerous given that women initiate the vast majority of divorces in the West—somewhere between 70% and 80% depending on the study.

The team at Essex and Missouri were right to highlight the higher dangers men tend to face daily at work too. Because of the jobs men are more likely to do, and are expected to do, they are 20 times more likely to have a fatal injury at work than women.[4] The 10 most dangerous jobs in the world are logging (132.7 deaths per 100,000), aircraft piloting and flight engineering (48.6), roofing (47), iron and steel work (32.5), mining (25.4), truck driving (24.3), farming and agricultural work (17.4), fishing (19.5), garbage and waste collection (30), and construction (9.4).[10] Overwhelmingly, these jobs are carried out by men. Indeed, although men make up half of America's workforce, they make up 90% of workplace fatalities.[11]

As the Essex and Missouri team also highlighted, men are far more likely to be called to serve their country in combat. 84% of soldiers in the military are male, and this feeds into a wider and more general notion that a man's life is more disposable than a woman's—something called the "Male Expendability Theory."[12] The theory says that from a reproductive standpoint, the lives of males are of less concern to a population than those of females because they are less necessary for population replacement. Therefore, any time a dangerous situation emerges with potential loss of life, men are expected to put themselves on the front-line. For example, when an intruder enters a family home, it's the man who is expected to confront them, putting his life at risk to defend those inside. Although this is not taught these days, traditionally, when a man and woman were walking side-by-side on a street pavement, the man was expected to walk road-side so that he would be the first to take the hit if any cars veered off-course. When the Titanic sank, 73% of women survived, but only 19% of men survived. This was due to the social convention that said women and children—their lives mattering more—should have priority access to the lifeboats. Indeed, whenever a tragedy is reported on the news that involves loss of life, special mention will still often be made whenever there are women and children involved. The inference being that if it were only men who had died, it would be a less sad or significant occasion.

Perhaps the most striking statistic that highlights the struggle men face is in regard to suicide. 74% of all suicides in the UK and 79% of all suicides in the US are committed by men and it's the second leading cause of death amongst young males in particular.[13]

Crossing The Sex Divide

The myth of male privilege has been laid-bare in recent years by some unlikely sources. Norah Vincent was a lesbian journalist who had been convinced for many years by the Woke idea that men are inherently more privileged and woman inherently more oppressed, and she intended to prove it by crossing the divide. Already possessing some traditionally masculine facial features, in 2003, she went "undercover" as a man called Ned with the intention to write a book about her experiences. She cut her hair short, hired a makeup artist to give her stubble, worked out to gain more muscle mass, and strapped her breasts to her chest. She even enlisted the help of a Julliard vocal coach to learn how to talk with a deeper voice.

After living as a man for eighteen months, she gave this report: "While all of us in the post-feminist movement are convinced that women have always had it worse and men have always had it better, it took me stepping into their shoes to realise that that's not true at all...My experience was one that made me feel very vulnerable and made me feel a lot of pain and difficulty." She says she felt alone and defeated as Ned. "Men are suffering. They have different problems than women have, but they don't have it better. They need our sympathy, they need our love, and they need each other more than anything else."[11]

Norah was so depressed by how difficult her life had been as a man that while writing her book, "Self-Made Man," she fell into a crippling depression and had to check into a mental facility. In the end, she was so broken by the experience which shattered her preconceptions and the basis of all she had once believed, that at the age of 53, she committed suicide. Living in the world from a man's perspective had been just too brutal.

In 2023, a transgender man (i.e. a woman who wants to present to the world as a man) went viral on social media when she spoke of similar struggles. She created a TikTok video describing how traumatic life had been in the eight years since she had gone through surgery. Fully transitioned with a low voice and beard, she said, "Nobody told me how lonely being a man is. I have had closer friendships with random women I met in the bathroom before I transitioned at clubs because of how open women are, than I've had in my eight years of transitioning." Through ensuing tears, she continued, "Before we [transgender men] transitioned, we knew what it was like to have people want to hug us, and have people want to talk to us, and have a community. And then you transition and you're just a guy walking down the street that people cross the street [to avoid] so that they're not near you. And friendships are so much harder to build. And people are colder [to men.] I now understand why the suicide rate is so much higher in men. Because this **** is lonely...I'm emotionally mature and I know how to build friendships and it is still really, really hard. Try to think about how you can, in your small little community reach out to the men in your life and help them feel seen for maybe a moment."[12]

The Woke, because of their adherence to Intersectionality and because they need it to be true to justify their hatred, will often declare that men are, by sheer virtue of their sex, always in a position of power and privilege, and that they have life so much easier. The reality is that men are no more privileged than women. Both sexes experience different challenges, face different hardships, and are each discriminated against in their own ways. In the majority of the countries of the world, as it turns out, men may actually have it harder.

3
THE WHITE PRIVILEGE MYTH

The idea of white privilege is also largely a myth. A widespread myth at that.

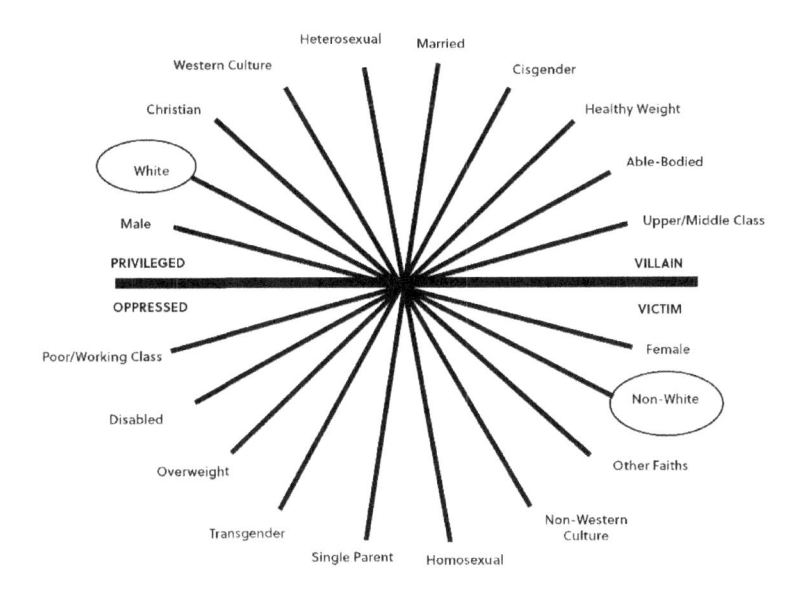

```
                    Heterosexual   Married
        Western Culture        Cisgender
            Christian            Healthy Weight
        ⟨White⟩                    Able-Bodied
            Male                 Upper/Middle Class
        PRIVILEGED                   VILLAIN
        ─────────────────────────────────────
        OPPRESSED                    VICTIM
        Poor/Working Class        Female
            Disabled            ⟨Non-White⟩
            Overweight          Other Faiths
                                Non-Western Culture
            Transgender
                Single Parent   Homosexual
```

In 2022, billboards started appearing around the United Kingdom which read in big capital letters, "HEY STRAIGHT WHITE MEN, PASS THE POWER!" They were designed by Woke artist, Nadina Ali, and paid for by the Artichoke Trust. In response, many white British men were confused. One responded on social media saying, "Which "straight white men" is this aimed at? What "power" is to be passed? To whom is the "power" to be passed?" Another said bluntly, "I have no power…[most] of us don't have an ounce of power we could give."[1]

Many white people would identify with this confusion. For example, in what way are poor white kids living on council estates, without fathers, surrounded by alcoholism and addiction privileged? How are they better off than anyone else in that position? Darren Grimes, a journalist who had such an upbringing, but who now works for GB News, was incensed by the billboards. He wrote, "I'm the grandson of a miner, the son of a single parent that was left on her own in a council estate to raise three children because my father was too interested in alcohol and Newcastle United to take some damn responsibility; I got my first job when I was 15, how dare these people talk about the need for us to recognise this racist notion? White privilege is a myth, and a divisive and dangerous myth at that."[2]

It is a myth, and the statistics make it clear. Not only are white British council estate kids no better off than others in the same position; the data suggests they might actually be worse off. According to the Department for Education, if you're a white British kid and are impoverished enough to qualify for free school meals, you are now part of the *least* likely group to go to university—less likely than any other race of child in the same position. Indeed, only 13% of white British boys on free school meals now go to university.[3] As early as 2015, the Institute for Fiscal Studies in England had reached a similar conclusion. They discovered that white British school pupils who were in the lowest socio-economic quintile were 10% less likely to participate in higher education than any other ethnic group in that same quintile.[4] The Department for Education also stated that white British kids "in general made less progress in England's schools in 2018 than Asians, blacks or Chinese."

The British government has known about this disparity for a long time but hasn't done anything about it. The reason being that if they do anything to help impoverished white children, they might be accused of racism. Kristina Murkett, writing for the Spectator, says, "We have sat on this data for years...[so] why have we not done anything about it so far?"[5] Mary Curnock Cook, the former head of The Universities and Colleges Admissions Service (UCAS) gives the answer saying that in her time, "this issue always got a few headlines but where it never got any traction at all was in policy-making in government...the subject of white boys is just too difficult for them." In other words, if the government does anything to help poor white boys—the group that now appears to need it the most—they will open themselves up to accusations of racism and sexism. So they are simply left to fail.

As an example of this, in 2018, the rap star Stormzy set up a scholarship fund to help black students gain access to Cambridge University. However, when Professor Sir Bryan Thwaites tried to make a point by approaching Winchester and Dulwich Colleges with an offer of scholarships for poor white boys, he was told this was discriminatory. Intersectionality has created this environment where ethnic minority kids can be helped along in life, but white kids can't. So again, it's fair to ask, under these circumstances, in which ways are these white kids privileged? As Kristina Murkett ends her Spectator article, "[We need to] get rid of the stigma over this issue...Forget culture wars; this is about children who need support, children who should have been prioritised but instead have been ignored because of pedantic politics and wokeness. Providing for one demographic group should not mean neglecting another, and we hardly need more proof that this is an urgent and pressing issue." Intersectionality has created an environment where we no longer help kids simply because they're kids. Instead, a great deal of focus is placed on the child's skin colour and that determines whether they get help or not. This has been divisive and dangerous.

The privilege myth reveals itself in other places; not just amongst children. For example, in 2016, it was discovered that white Americans had a median household income of $67,865, which was lower than Indonesian Americans ($71,616), Pakistani Americans ($72,389), Malaysian Americans ($72,443), Sri Lankan Americans ($73,865), Filipino Americans ($84,620), Taiwanese Americans ($90,122) and Indian Americans ($110,026).[3] The same sort of picture exists in the UK where for example 42% of Indian households have a weekly income of £1000 or more, while 26% of white British households have a weekly income of the same amount.

What About Everything Else?

Even when white people, and white men in particular do succeed, to claim that it's only due to an inherently biased power structure is overly simplistic, cynical, and uncharitable. It ignores everything else that goes into achievement, such as character, hard work, determination, and good decision-making.

In 2014, when this idea of systemic white male privilege was first starting to gain traction in the mainstream media, a white male Princeton student called Tal Fortang wrote a piece for Time Magazine to explain how demeaning it is to be told that everything he or his family had achieved was merely down to the colour of his skin. He wrote about his family history and asked which part of it could be considered privileged saying, "I have uncarthed some examples of the privilege with which my family was blessed, and now I think I better understand those who assure me that skin colour allowed my family and I to flourish today.

Perhaps it's the privilege my grandfather and his brother had to flee their home as teenagers when the Nazis invaded Poland, leaving their mother and five young siblings behind, running and running until they reached a Displaced Persons camp in Siberia, where they would do years of hard labour in the bitter cold until World War II ended…Perhaps it was the privilege my great-grandmother and those five great-aunts and uncles I never knew had of being shot into an open grave outside their hometown. Maybe that's my privilege. Or maybe it's the privilege my grandmother had of spending weeks upon weeks on a death march through Polish forests in subzero temperatures, one of just a handful to survive, only to be put in Bergen-Belsen concentration camp where she would have died but for the Allied forces who liberated her and helped her regain her health when her weight dwindled to barely 80 pounds.

Perhaps my privilege is that those two resilient individuals came to came to America with no money and no English, obtained citizenship, learned the language and met each other; that my grandfather started a humble wicker basket business with nothing but long hours, an idea, and an iron will—to paraphrase the man I never met: 'I escaped Hitler. Some business troubles are going to ruin me?' Maybe my privilege is that they worked hard enough to raise four children, and to send them to Jewish day school and eventually City College.

Perhaps it was my privilege that my own father worked hard enough in City College to earn a spot at a top graduate school, got a good job, and for 25 years got up well before the crack of dawn, sacrificing precious time he wanted to spend with those he valued most—his wife and kids—to earn that living. I can say with certainty there was no legacy involved in any of his accomplishments. The wicker business just isn't that influential. Now would you say that we've been really privileged? That our success has been gift-wrapped?

That's the problem with calling someone out for the "privilege" which you assume has defined their narrative. You don't know what their struggles have been, what they may have gone through to be where they are. Assuming they've benefitted from "power systems" or other conspiratorial imaginary institutions denies them credit for all they've done, things of which you may not even conceive. You don't know whose father died defending your freedom. You don't know whose mother escaped oppression. You don't know who conquered their demons, or may still be conquering them now."

Fortang is correct. There are other reasons than a person's sex or colour of their skin why they may have succeeded. There's hard work, there's good decision-making, there's sacrifice. This is ultimately what matters most and it's what the Intersectional Theory misses by over-simplifying. It creates a flawed narrative and warped perspective that says personal histories don't matter. Character counts for nothing. Individual grit, perseverance, decisions and faith makes no difference. Because our whole lives are merely predetermined by the colour of our skin and nothing else. This not only is offensive to those who have had to struggle to get where they are, but it's disempowering to people of other skin colours, who are told there is simply nothing they can do to succeed because of these power systems. And it's simply untrue. As we just highlighted, Americans of Indonesian, Malaysian, Sri Lankan, Indian, Pakistani, Taiwanese and Filipino backgrounds are all now earning more on average than white Americans.

The bottom line here is that, to automatically hate people because they have achieved in life, on the assumption they only did so because they had it handed to them on a plate, is cynical and wrong. It means that successful people often become the subject of hatred simply for having done the right things, or because they came from a family who did the right things. As I said before, Intersectional Theory is problematic for encouraging a witch-hunt style hatred of anyone, but it's even worse that the hatred is often levelled against people for such unfair and superficial reasons.

4
INVERTING STATUS

Apart from encouraging hatred for spurious reasons, another problem with Intersectional Theory is that it has inverted the path to social status.

The Path to Status

For all recorded history, and in all cultures, the way to achieve high status has traditionally been to become accomplished—to achieve something of note. Think of celebrated individuals from the past. Why do we revere William Shakespeare? Because of his accomplishments with the English language. Likewise, we celebrate Mozart for his accomplishments with music; Newton for his accomplishments in science; and Churchill for his accomplishments in wartime leadership. Long-time followers of The Fuel Project will know that my own biggest hero outside the Bible is William Wilberforce, who I revere because of his accomplishments in using Christian principles to reform British society.

Now here's the thing—accomplishment is difficult. If you want to accomplish something great, you're going to have to become competent in a particular field. And if you want to become competent in anything at all, it's going to require a lot of practice, effort, sacrifice and struggle. Now it's as you struggle towards the competence necessary for achievement that your character is then going to be developed. The Bible tells us about this. In Romans we read, "We can rejoice too, when we run into problems and trials, for we know that they help us to develop endurance. And endurance develops strength of character…" (Romans 5:3-5) Struggle develops character. As you strive for your goal, there are going to be some days when it doesn't look like you'll make it. There are going to be obstacles, frustrations, setbacks and disappointments. You're probably going to have to contend with nay-sayers and perhaps you'll want to give up. But if you really are determined to achieve something great, you won't give up. You'll find a way to dig deep, to battle through, and to keep going.

Almost everyone we revere went through this kind of struggle. Walt Disney became famed for his accomplishments in entertainment but he was once fired from a junior animation job at the Kansas City Star because his editor believed he "lacked imagination and had no good ideas."[1] Albert Einstein is perhaps the most recognised scientist in history but he was once told in a school report card that "he would never amount to anything."[2] Charlotte Bronte is a literary giant but was once told by her school teacher that she wrote "indifferently" and "knows nothing of grammar." Abraham Lincoln is one of America's greatest statesmen but he experienced defeat in several campaigns for public office before eventually becoming sixteenth President of the United States. Steven Spielberg—perhaps the world's most successful movie director—was rejected three times from the University of Southern California School of Theater, Film and Television. Claude Monet—one of the most celebrated artists in history—was mocked and rejected by the Parisian artistic elite. Michael Jordan—perhaps basketball's greatest ever player—was cut from his high school basketball team. We revere all these people for their accomplishments now but the truth is, to reach their goals, they had to struggle. They had to work through the setbacks and defeats and in the process, their character was refined. They had to learn humility, empathy, dedication, hard work, discipline, resilience and courage. This, in truth, is really why we celebrate high achievers and award them social status. It's partly because of what they achieved, but it's more because we understand the kind of person they needed to have been to achieve it.

I admire Wilberforce for reforming British society and ending slavery in the British Empire but the reason he's so inspirational to me is because I know the kind of character he needed to have to achieve that goal. If he'd had the power to do it merely by signing a piece of paper, it would still have been the right thing to do and I would think well of him for making that decision, but I wouldn't revere him quite so much. What I really admire—what I find so inspirational—is how he persisted even when all hope seemed lost. I admire his diligence, even through bouts of ill-health and poor eyesight. I admire his resilience even when friends abandoned him. I admire his courage to stand alone in parliament and be a lone voice in the crowd, even when that crowd tried to drown him out. That's what makes him worthy of high status in my eyes—the person he needed to be to achieve the goal. The character he developed through the struggle. If I walked into a room in the early 19th Century and Wilberforce was there and he began talking, I would want to listen to him for those reasons.

Now rewarding achievement with status generally works well for society. It means that people will generally strive to become the kind of individuals who achieve i.e. competent individuals of good character. And yes, if they reach their goal, along with high status, they will probably also find themselves with power, influence and wealth. These things tend to follow success. When they do, they're often deserved.

The Inversion

Inverting Status

When Intersectional Theory came along however, it inverted the path to status. Now, the way to achieve it is not through accomplishment, but through *victimhood*. You don't want to find yourself above the horizontal line in any respect; you want to find yourself below it. You want to be able to demonstrate that you are in an oppressed category—whether that be you are in a position of physical weakness, poverty or are part of some marginalised minority group. Those are the ones who the Woke will celebrate and champion and revere.

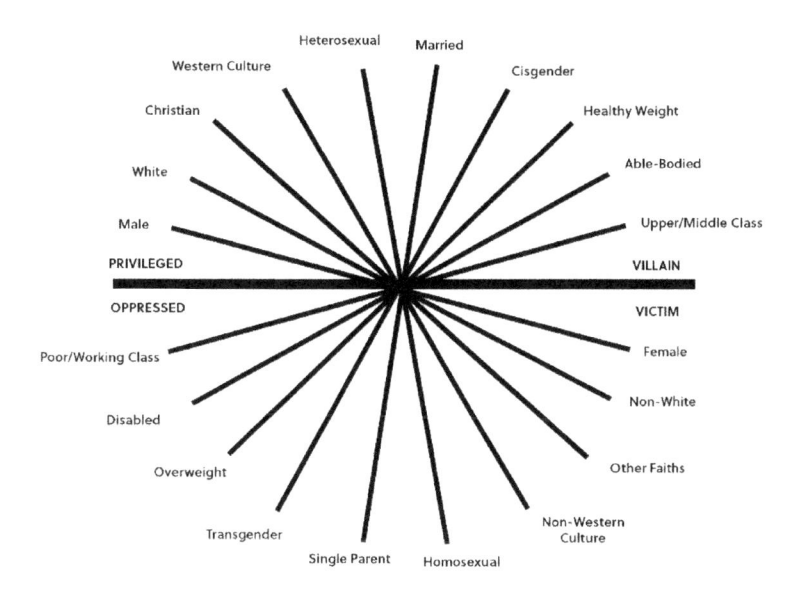

If you want status amongst the Woke there's no need to strive for competence and no need to develop the character necessary for great things…simply be female. Or be non-white. Be non-Christian; be poor; be a single parent; be overweight; be homosexual; transgender; or disabled. Anything you can claim below the horizontal line will get you attention and the more loudly you can shout about your oppression, the more attention and adulation you will receive. As I already mentioned in the first chapter, the more oppression points you can score, the more feted you will be. If you're a *woman*, you will have some status. If you're a *black* woman, you will have more. If you're a black, *lesbian* woman, even more still. And in the same way power, influence and wealth traditionally followed high status individuals for *accomplishment* under the old system; those same things will follow high status individuals for *victimhood* under this one. For example, if you're a black, lesbian, woman who makes a big noise about your oppression, platforms and opportunities will start to open up. There will be jobs and financial support too. The Woke will want to hear your story and to champion your cause. They will hang on your every word. We'll get into the specifics of the benefits of victimhood over the next few chapters but the point I'm trying to make here is that you no longer actually have to *do* anything to get the benefits. No longer do you have to accomplish something, and therefore, no longer do you have to become the kind of person who accomplishes something. In other words, no longer do you have to be the kind of person who struggles towards competence, and whose character becomes refined by that struggle. Now, all you have to be is…a woman. Or a black woman. Or an lesbian black woman. It's far easier. Instead of having to make something of yourself and do difficult things and refine your character, now you simply have to signal about how oppressed and discriminated against you are and the doors will begin open. The more loudly you complain, the more opportunities will arise.

If rewarding people with high status for *achievement* worked well for society because it encouraged people to be the kind of people who might achieve, this new framework now produces the opposite effect. As we reward people with status for *victimhood* it encourages people to be victims. Today then, because of the influence of Intersectional Theory, we have a rush of people not striving for achievement or character development, but actively striving for victimhood. Essentially, striving to cry, whinge, wail, and complain the loudest so that the Woke might revere them and celebrate them.

5
THE VICTIMHOOD OLYMPICS

There's a famous Scottish poem by Walter Wingate that will help us understand what happens when we actively reward victimhood. It's called "The Sair Finger." I had to learn it when I was about nine-years-old as part of a school poetry recital competition and generations of school children from Scotland have done the same. I'll copy the original Scots version first and then write an English translation. To get an idea of what's happening here as you read, it's about a young boy called John who's got a splinter in his finger. Looking for some sympathy, he goes to his mum. The poem is written from her perspective.

THE SAIR FINGER
(Original Scots)

You've hurt your finger? Puir wee man!
Your pinkie? Deary me!
Noo, jist you haud it 'at wye till
I get my specs and see!
My, so it is–and there's the skelf!
Noo, dinna greet nae mair.
See there–my needle's gotten't oot!
I'm sure that wisnae sair?
An' noo, tae mak it hale the morn,
Pit on a wee bit saw,

And tie a bonnie hankie roon't
Noo, there na–rin awa'!
Your finger sair ana'? You rogue,
You're only lettin' on.
Weel, weel, then–see noo, there ye are,
Row'd up the same as John!

(English Translation)

You've hurt your finger? Poor little man!
Your pinkie? Oh dear!
Now, just you hold it that way till
I get my glasses and see!
My, so it is–and there's the splinter!
Now don't cry anymore
See there–my needle has gotten it out
I'm sure that wasn't sore?
And now to make it heal tomorrow,
I'll put on a little bit of salve,
And tie a nice handkerchief round it
Now, there–now run away!
Your finger sore as well? You rogue,
You're only pretending.
Well, well, then–see now, there you are,
Bandaged up the same as John![1]

So here's little Johnny who has become a victim of a splinter in his finger. He comes to show his mum who very naturally begins to shower him with sympathy. She starts fussing over him. "You've hurt your finger? Oh dear! You poor thing!" She puts her glasses on, manages to get the splinter out, puts on some salve, and uses her handkerchief to bandage it up. In truth, she probably gives him more attention than the splinter really warrants—splinters generally don't require bandages—but nevertheless she wants him to feel indulged with love.

Somewhere in the background, there's an unnamed, presumably younger brother, who's overhearing this and it makes him jealous. He wants that kind of love and attention as well. He thinks to himself, "How do I get mum to fuss over me in the same way?" He decides there's only one solution…if he wants to share in the kind of affection his brother just experienced, he needs to become a victim of the same kind of sore finger his brother just had. And yet, there's a catch. He doesn't actually have a sore finger. His finger is unfortunately splinter-free.

He hatches a plan and decides there's only one thing for it. He's going to have to fake it. He walks into the room and the amateur dramatics begin. "Me too! Me too!" he shouts. "I have a splinter in my finger as well! It's in such terrible pain! Oh, the pain! Woe is me for I am undone!" Something like that. He grasps for victimhood.

Now the mum, for her part, can clearly see there's nothing wrong with the brother. But because she understands his motivation—that he just wants to feel special like John—she decides to indulge him. She goes along with the charade and panders to him. She pretends to take an imaginary splinter out of his finger, puts some salve on it, and bandages him up just the same as his brother.

This poem teaches us an essential truth, which is that when there's status, love, compassion, attention, sympathy, money or indeed any kind of benefit available for victimhood, you're going to inspire people to rush to claim it for themselves. Indeed, people will even fake victimhood if it means they get to share in some of these rewards.

There's a law of economics which says, "whatever you subsidise, you will get more of." If you reward victimhood, you'll get more of it. We saw this law in effect during the Covid-19 debacle. In March 2020, the British government announced the furlough scheme, which stated that if people could prove their income had been negatively affected by lockdowns, the Treasury would pay them compensation of any amount up to their normal monthly wage. When people realised free money was being dished out to victims of the virus, well…it caused a rush of people claiming they were victims of the virus. Even when they weren't. It's estimated that during the couple of years that the furlough scheme was running in the UK, around £5 billion was paid out to fraudulent claims.[2]

Me Too

The "Me Too" movement is another example of this mechanism. In 2017, two New York Times journalists called Jodi Kantor and Megan Twohey revealed they had been sexually abused by the American film producer, Harvey Weinstein. These women were telling the truth about their victimhood and were rightly showered with compassion for their ordeal. They were given high status too. They were offered media platforms where they could tell their stories—including a book deal. They were celebrated, feted, showered with compliments for their bravery in speaking up, and they, along with the rest of his genuine victims were compensated financially from a fund totalling $17 million.[3]

Following these revelations, the actress Alyssa Milano encouraged women from all walks of life to share their own stories of sexual harassment on Twitter (now X) using the hashtag #metoo. As thousands of genuine victims flooded forward, they too were rightly given status, sympathy, compassion, support, a platform to tell their stories, and they were showered with praise for their courage.

In the passing of time however, "The Sair Finger" mechanism began to kick in. Many women saw the benefits that were being given to these victims and decided they would like those things too. Even though they were not genuine victims, they tried to paint themselves as though they were, and the stories began to become increasingly fanciful. For example, some women claimed they were a victim of sexual harassment because a man had merely flirted with them clumsily. Some claimed they were a victim of sexual harassment because a man had asked them out on a date more than once. In 2017, the Pulitzer Prize winning writer, Stephen Henderson, was fired from his job at The Free Press because he made a couple of rejected passes at a co-worker outside of work. She claimed that it "made her uncomfortable,"[4] and therefore she was a victim of sexual harassment. While she was lavished with praise for her courage in enduring the horror of being asked out on a date twice by the same man, Henderson was professionally destroyed. Other women claimed—and this notably led to a change of workplace policy at Netflix in 2018—that being looked at by a man for more than five seconds made them a victim of sexual harassment as well.[5] It began to get ludicrous. But in a world where victimhood is so rewarded, the rush was on to claim it in any way possible.

The race to claim victimhood in the Postmodern world has become so extreme that it's been dubbed, "The Victimhood Olympics."

At times it can feel like there is a competition on, where they who whine the loudest win the biggest prizes. And so it's reduced large swathes of society to behaving like toddlers. Have you ever seen toddlers getting into an argument and when one begins to cry, the other suddenly realises that if he doesn't cry too, the parents will assume he's the villain and lavish comfort on his opponent? So they enter into a crying match, each one trying to wail louder and pull a sadder face than the other, in the hope that when an adult inevitably rushes onto the scene, they'll each be seen as the victim and win the cuddles. That's a bit like what's happening under the Intersectional framework. Everyone trying to out-tantrum the others to claim the highest honours.

There's a very old comedy sketch from the 1960s involving John Cleese and Graham Chapman of Monty Python fame. It's called "The Four Yorkshiremen" and it involves four characters competing with one another to establish who had been the victim of the most impoverished childhood. As the conversation goes on, the claims get increasingly exaggerated. Cleese's character starts by saying that when he was a child, "We had nothing. We lived in a tiny, tumbled down old house, with great holes in the roof." Chapman's character interjects, "House?? You used to have a house? We used to live in one room—twenty-six of us—no furniture, half the floor was missing, and we were all huddled in one corner for fear of falling." The third man steps in: "Room?? You were lucky to have a room! We used to have to live in the corridor." The fourth chimes in: "A corridor? I used to dream of living in a corridor. That would have been a palace to us! We used to live in a water tank on the rubbish tip. Every morning we'd be woken up by a load of rotting fish dumped on us. House?! Huh!" Cleese's character sees that he's been outdone in the victimhood stakes and comes back into the conversation swinging: "Well, when I said 'house', I mean it was only a hole in the ground covered by a couple of foot of torn canvas, but it was a house to us!" The competition to establish who had the toughest childhood keeps getting more wild until eventually they're talking about waking up in the morning "at half past ten at night, half an hour before they'd gone to bed," "eating a lump of poison for breakfast," and "working 29 hour days."

This sketch is a metaphor for our times. Realising that status and its trappings are won through victimhood, the competition is on to establish who has been the most hard-done-by in life and the claims can often get ludicrous. Indeed, you will often see people today craving victimhood so much, that they will deliberately try to **manufacture** it for themselves. Perhaps the best example I can think of here, because for a while it became a social media trend, was where young women would put on the most revealing clothing possible, go to the gym, and record themselves working out, in the hope some man would interact with them, or at least just glance in their general direction. If anyone did, they would post the video to social media shouting, "me too! Me too! I too have been the victim of sexual harassment!" These women did it in the hope that it would win them sympathy, compassion, status, clicks, likes, and possibly platform to share their stories.

Overall, this rush for victimhood doesn't make for a productive or happy society. Instead of striving to work hard, overcome setbacks and achieve like under the old system, we're now just encouraging people to wallow in self-pity, to complain and to throw tantrums. Embracing the ideas of Intersectional Theory has infantilised us, made us less resilient, and turned us into toddlers.

6
THE BENEFITS OF VICTIMHOOD

But oh, the benefits of victimhood are just so addictive. The prizes are just so good. Status and platform, you see, aren't the only trophies on offer. You will also be given carte blanche to behave however you wish.

Carte Blanche

Imagine you're at a dinner party and you meet someone who is particularly rude. They're unpleasant, obnoxious and aggressive. Under normal circumstances you would hold that person accountable for their behaviour, but imagine the host takes you to the side and explains, "please excuse Jeff. He just lost his brother to cancer last week." Doesn't that change everything? Jeff's a victim of tragic circumstances so he is indeed excused. He's off the hook. He has carte blanche. Nothing he says or does at the moment will be held against him.

We saw something like this happening when George Floyd was killed by Minnesotan police officers in 2020. The Black Lives Matter (BLM) organisation began whipping up crowds, claiming that Floyd was symbolic of the kind of persecution black people across the United States face every day. After stoking a sense of shared victimhood, thousands of people nationwide began rampaging around city streets, smashing up windows, destroying property, and looting businesses. As they committed vandalism, arson and theft, it wasn't held against them. The Woke left-wing media in particular sympathised. It was deemed that these people, being victims, were entitled in that moment to behave however they wished. They had carte blanche. Instead of arresting the unruly mobs, the police were seen begging for forgiveness and taking a knee at their feet.

When others around the world, and especially in the United Kingdom, saw these riots taking place, "The Sair Finger" reflex kicked in still further. Even though the George Floyd event happened in another country, on another continent, and had nothing to do with the British police force or British government at all, many saw how claiming victimhood would give them carte blanche to vandalise and loot with impunity in this country too. This was their chance, not only to steal a lot of free merchandise from shops—sneakers, clothes and TVs—but instead of being jailed for it, you would be feted for it! They had carte blanche! And so it was that many people in Britain began ludicrously claiming that they were somehow also victims of Minnesotan police brutality, and were therefore also justified in a criminal rampage. The full buffoonery of this moment was demonstrated when the British protestors copied the American chant, "hands up, don't shoot!" The reason this is so silly is because the British police force, as a matter of course, don't actually carry guns. Nevertheless, the Woke establishment largely sympathised with British BLM rioters, and just like their American counterparts, British police officers began kneeling before the criminals asking for forgiveness. Even though it was nothing to do with them.

Evading Justice

Speaking of evading justice, in November, 2021, a British Member of Parliament called Claudia Webbe—a black woman—was charged with harassment when it was discovered she was bombarding a love rival called Michelle Merritt with threatening phone calls and messages.

During the campaign of intimidation, she threatened to permanently disfigure Merritt by throwing acid over her. She also threatened to released naked photos of Merritt to her family.

When Webbe was brought to court to face justice, she repeatedly tried to use her sex and skin colour to claim victimhood so that she might be excused. She said, "I am a black woman in a white court, facing a white system and white persecutors. I have been deliberately targeted because I am vulnerable. I know first-hand the sexism and racism institutions and media use to vilify black women."[1] This calculated line of argument gained much sympathy with the Woke court and she was actually given an extremely lenient suspended sentence. She had rather effectively used her identity to evade justice.

Jobs and Platforms

Unique jobs and platforms are available if you can claim victimhood too. It's now become commonplace for companies to hire "Diversity, Equality and Inclusion Officers," whose job it is to make sure their organisation can't be held liable for discrimination. These roles are generally always filled by people who belong to a perceived oppressed class, and the salaries tend to be extremely generous. In the UK for example, the average salary for a diversity officer at the time of writing is £45,000-£51,000, which is above the nationwide average of £33,402. At the top end, these salaries can even extend up to around £230,000. Indeed, it was reported on 18th September, 2021, that Prerana Issar, the diversity tsar for the British National Health Service (NHS), was earning that very amount, making her more highly paid than even the NHS CEO, who earned £35,000 less.[2] At the time, it meant she was even earning around double the amount of then Prime Minister, Boris Johnson.

Many companies will now openly insist that job openings and promotion opportunities are only available to people from a perceived oppressed class. In June 2021, the BBC banned white people from applying for jobs on two of their shows—Springwatch and The One Show.[3] In June 2023, the Royal Air Force (RAF) had some internal emails leaked that revealed they were deliberately ignoring pilot applications from white men. Instead, to fulfil diversity quotas, they were looking to fast-track people from minority backgrounds and women. The correspondence from a squadron leader read, "I notice that the boards have recently been predominantly white male heavy. If we don't have enough BAME (Black And Minority Ethnic) and female to board then we need to make the decision to pause boarding and seek more BAME and female from the recruitment force. I don't really need to see loads of useless white male pilots..."[4] So much for white male privilege.

When there are jobs being created specifically for people who can claim victimhood; when they are extremely well paid; and when you know you'll be fast-tracked through the ranks of many organisations for being one of these perceived victims, it only amplifies the desire to be one. And again, this is where the "Sair Finger" reflex comes in.

In 2015, a white, blonde-haired woman called Rachel Dolezal made the headlines when it was discovered that she had for many years, been pretending to be black to reap the financial and societal rewards. Having darkened her skin and frizzed her hair, she became renowned as an outspoken and respected black activist. Of course, with that identity had come many new opportunities. She had been given a job as the President of the National Association for the Advancement of Colored People (NAACP) and the chair of Spokane's police ombudsman commission. She was given a local newspaper column and a job as a lecturer at Eastern Washington University. However, when a local TV news crew arrived one afternoon to interview her, the reporter asked her straight, "Are you African American?" Dolezal froze and replied, "I don't understand the question." The reporter re-phrased the question: "Are your parents white?" At that point, Dolezal turned from the camera and fled. When it was discovered she wasn't an Intersectional victim at all, she lost it all. Her status and standing in the community was destroyed; her job at the university, her job with the NACCP and her job with police commission was gone. Her newspaper column was taken from her too.

When your status and salary depends on victimhood, people will likely make sure they are perceived as victims. There's a quote that goes along the lines of, "never trust someone to solve a problem whose salary depends on it not being solved." When diversity officers are given huge salaries to fix diversity problems in an organisation, they will make sure the supposed diversity problem never is fixed. Because the moment it is fixed, that's the moment their role becomes obsolete. They will always say that more that needs to be done. There will always be some imagined inequality that hasn't quite been resolved. If an organisation hires a diversity officer, you can guarantee that organisation will always have a "problem" with diversity.

What's The Motivation To Leave Victimhood Behind?

When we understand the many perks that victimhood now bestows, we understand why so many are clamouring to claim it. And indeed the question must be asked, "within this climate, even for genuine victims, what motivation could people have to leave that identity behind?" If victimhood is now the path to status, respect, position, platform, power, jobs, wealth, carte blanche, and even justice evasion, why would anyone ever give it up? Why wouldn't they determine to hold onto victimhood even when they could let it go?

I once spoke to a pastor who ran a drop-in centre for drug addicts. In this place, called "The Lighthoose," people were offered a free facility where they could come for warmth, food, friendship, conversation, counselling and prayer. I believe there may also have been money available to them through a government grant if they could claim to be part of the recovery program there, although I'm not sure about that. What I do know is that when I visited The Lighthoose one dark, winter evening, they were enjoying a cosy weekly Bible study full of camaraderie, Pepsi and free pizza.

During a conversation I had with that pastor, he said something that has remained with me. He told of how easy it was to get drug addicts 99% of the way towards recovery but that the last 1% could often be near impossible. He said the addicts understand that they only get these benefits as long as they are considered a victim of addiction. The moment they are fully recovered, they are expected to take full responsibility for their lives again and all the perks stop. There's no valid reason for them to keep visiting The Lighthoose anymore. Which means they miss out on the free warmth, food, friendship, conversation, counselling and prayer. No more financial support and government grants. No more free pizza! Instead, it's time for them to go get a job and start running their own affairs. The pastor said that when faced with the prospect of losing the perks of their victimhood, getting jobs and making their own way in the world again, they would often deliberately *choose* to relapse.

There's a relevant story in the Bible where Jesus met a disabled man by the pool of Bethesda. This man had been lying by the pool for thirty-eight years and the Bible says, "When Jesus saw him and knew he had been ill for a long time, he asked him, 'Would you like to get well?'" (John 5:5-6) That seems like an unusual question. Of course a disabled man would like to get well! Wouldn't he? Who would want to remain a victim of disability when they're being offered the chance to walk? Well, what Jesus understood was that when someone has been a victim for a long time, they can get used to the advantages. After all, if this man were to be healed, he would have to take responsibility for his life. He would have to get a job and support himself. No more free handouts from passers-by.

This is a problem we see in this age of Intersectional Theory then. The perks encourage people to claim victimhood when they aren't, but furthermore, it encourages people to wallow in victimhood even when they have been one, but could now realistically move on and leave the identity behind.

7
ENFEEBLED

Why is it important that genuine victims should eventually leave the identity behind? Well, because if they don't, they will become disempowered and enfeebled.

When Compassion Enfeebles

I remember a time in childhood—I was perhaps around six-years-old—when I contracted the flu. You could say I was a victim of the flu. I really was. I felt terrible. When my mum saw my condition and felt my temperature, much to my delight, she insisted I stay off school. For the rest of the day, I lay in my comfortable bed and was waited on hand-and-foot. My every whim was catered to, food and drink was brought on demand, and for a time I lived like a king. I confess that I loved wallowing in the sympathy and compassion that contracting the flu had afforded me.

As the days passed however, I was horrified to discover I was gradually getting better. I realised that if the flu disappeared completely, I'd have to give up this life of ease, get out of bed, and go back to school! I have to admit that when faced with such a prospect, I tried to make that flu last for as long as possible. Indeed, I ended up pushing it too far. Every morning my mum would ask if I was ready to go back to school yet and every morning I'd insist I still felt a bit off. After many days of this routine, and with my terrible child acting beginning to falter, my mum's patience finally expired. She told me she knew I'd recovered and was faking—indeed that I had been faking for several days already—and that I was going back to school that instant!

Although I didn't enjoy it at the time, that withdrawal of compassion from my mum, and the subsequent kick in the butt was the best thing for me. I had been genuinely sick and initially compassion was the right response. However, if my mum had continued pandering to my sense of victimhood even when I was able to go back to school, the compassion would have become counter-productive. I'd have wallowed in self-pity and stayed in bed much longer than necessary. I'd have missed important classes. My educational and social development would have been stunted. Physically, my body would have suffered by staying in bed all the time too. I'd have become lazy and conditioned to dependence. As brutal as it may sound, the day came when the best thing for me was to be told to quit whining; quit feeling sorry for myself; and get back out into the world.

That is the case more generally. The best thing for all of us—even when we have been a genuine victim—is to be offered the minimal amount of compassion necessary. Anything beyond that becomes counter-productive. As soon as possible, genuine victims need to be told to quit whining and wallowing in self-pity, to stop making excuses, stop clinging to the victimhood identity; to stop looking at what we think we can't do and push through to see what we can do, even in spite of the circumstances.

I think here again of the drug addicts at The Lighthoose, deliberately choosing to relapse into victimhood so they could keep the perks. It's not good to keep pandering to that. As long as their sense of victimhood is eternally affirmed with sympathy and free handouts, victims is what they will remain. They will deliberately choose to stay dependent on programs like The Lighthoose and become enfeebled by the endless compassion. Disempowered. What they really need is for someone to push them into a different mindset. If they *can* stand on their own two feet, they ***should*** stand on their own two feet.

There's a story that Jordan Peterson told in one of his old lectures. He said, "People say, 'I could never be brutal', but you can kill people with compassion, no problem. There's a rule of thumb in nursing homes that I also use to guide my interactions with my children and my clients…and people in general. The rule is, 'Do not do anything for anyone that they can do themselves.' If you do something for someone they could do themselves, you steal from them. Imagine you're working with really elderly people who have Alzheimer's. It might be easier to do something for them than to let them struggle through it, but you will just speed their demise by taking away the last vestiges of their independence. It's the same thing with kids. It's like, 'struggle through it, man!'

Did you ever see, 'My Left Foot?' That's a great movie. It's about this author in Ireland who had cerebral palsy, and all he could really do was use his left foot. That was it. The rest of him was pretty spastic and not controllable. But he was there mentally. He was very intelligent. And his dad would ***not*** help him. For example, he had to drag himself up the stairs with just his left foot. His dad just would not help him. And what happened was…he learned how to live…you know…he could function. And the movie does a lovely job of laying that out, but you have to be one hard-hearted son-of-a-***** to let your son crawl up the stairs with his left foot over and over. Think about that. But what's the alternative? If he would have been catered to, he would have ended up just like someone…you would expect who had always been catered to."[1]

Imagine someone says, "I really wish I could play the piano but I had a stroke when I was younger." There are two responses to that. The first is what you may think to be the compassionate response. You could say something like, "aww yes, you'll never be able to play the piano. It's so sad. You poor thing." In which case you would affirm their sense of victimhood and encourage them to wallow in self-pity. The other response may seem harsh but you could say, "what makes you think you can't play the piano even with the stroke? Stop wallowing in self-pity and try." Because what if they could? Of course their stroke would make it harder for them—that's undeniable—but what if they *could* struggle through and do it? If you pandered to them as a victim forever and affirmed their sense of helplessness, they would never fulfil their potential. They would never learn the piano. At some point, it would be far more empowering to withdraw the compassion, to tell them to stop seeing themselves as a helpless victim, to stop wallowing in self-pity, and to stop using it as an excuse not to try. As a rule of thumb, there should always be a limit on compassion for victims because at some point it will enfeeble the very ones you're trying to help, and keep them pinned down.

There's another relevant Jordan Peterson lecture where he's discussing raising his daughter, who had a lot of problems with illness in childhood. He says, "My daughter had a lot of illnesses when she was adolescent and they were very serious. It was very difficult to figure out what to do about that because you couldn't exactly apply normative rules. We always had to figure out when she was communicating her symptoms to us, how seriously to take those. And the answer was, 'the least amount of serious possible.' Because we needed to know and she needed to know what she could do in spite of the fact she had problems. One of the things I really tried to instil in her is that you don't ever want to use your illness as an excuse for not doing anything. Sometimes when you're not feeling well, you can do more than you think. Sometimes there's a temptation that flits through your mind where you think, 'I don't really want to do that and I'm not feeling very well, so I don't have to do it.' If you do that a hundred times, then you don't know how sick you are anymore. And then you're in real trouble, because not only are you sick, but you've muddied the waters. You now have two problems…you're actually ill and you've betrayed yourself by using that as an excuse not to pursue your responsibilities."[2]

A significant problem of Wokeness is that it doesn't put a limit on the compassion. Instead, it only ever encourages people to amplify their victimhood. Indeed, it tells them to make victimhood their whole identity. And then showers them with endless perks and status for it. Therefore, over the long-term, it enfeebles the very people it claims to be trying to help. Let's say for example that a woman wants to do something but she finds being a woman makes it more difficult. You can play to that sense of victimhood by offering her endless sympathy and you can reinforce the idea that her womanhood is a barrier to success. But with that attitude, she will never get anywhere. Alternatively—and this is better thing to do—you can say, "you know what, maybe it is more difficult being a woman and maybe it isn't. But unless you stop playing the victim, stop using this as an excuse, and start struggling to achieve, you're definitely never going to get anywhere." It's brutal to say that to someone who feels hard-done-by but it's that kick in the butt that moves them from a place of self-pity to empowerment.

The same thing goes for the black community. If you constantly tell people that their skin colour makes something impossible and the whole world is against them, you engender a sense of hopelessness that enfeebles and keeps them down. Zee Powell is a black South African woman who went to Cambridge University. She says that when she arrived in England to study, she was encouraged to join black societies that filled her head with ideas of Intersectional oppression. She says being told she was unable to succeed because of the colour of her skin stripped her of agency and made her feel powerless. She was enfeebled. She says, "I definitely, especially when I was at university, felt that. I was in constant despair. I didn't know what to do with myself. I didn't know how I was going to navigate the world because what was the point? What was the point in trying to do things when inevitably I'm going to fail because I'm black, and the systems and institutions are against me? And you end up fulfilling that prophecy in yourself. It was so unhealthy for me."[3] In the passing of time, she was able to free herself from that victim mentality and by entering into the real world, she discovered that actually she could achieve just the same as anyone else. She just had to stop wallowing in self-pity.

    The truth is that everyone knows what it's like to be a victim of something. Yes even straight white men, as we have already seen. We all have our struggles. We've all experienced illness, injustices, or the deaths of loved ones. We've likely all known what it's like to be bullied or mocked. There's a time in those moments where it's absolutely the right thing to do to accept you are a victim of something and receive compassion. In those moments, it's absolutely the right response of those around you to give it. However, those who succeed in life are the ones who refuse to get comfortable in that identity. They hold the victim label for not one second longer than is absolutely necessary.

I once saw an interview with Patrice Evra, the ex-professional footballer who starred for Manchester United, Juventus and France. Upon the release of his autobiography he talked about the racist abuse he received in his career as a black player, and more specifically about the sexual abuse he received from a teacher when he was aged thirteen. Patrice Evra was a genuine victim. However, he said, "I prefer to be an inspiration to people and an example rather than a victim. I don't want that role of victim even if the truth is I have been a victim." Evra understood that as soon as you embrace that role, you are disempowering yourself and allowing yourself to be pinned down by circumstances. He would rather not let those events define him or diminish the person he could become. Instead, he pushed on to discover what he was capable of. Consequently, Evra became an English Premier League champion with Manchester United five times over. He also won the European Champions League, the FIFA Club World Cup, the English League Cup (x3), the Italian league with Juventus (x3), Italian Cup (x2), Italian Super Cup, French League Cup with Monaco. It was better to do that than wallow in self-pity wailing that his skin colour made success impossible.

This is another problem with Intersectional Theory then—that it encourages people in certain sub-categories to see themselves as eternal victims, simply because of the things like the colour of their skin, or their sex. In entrenches them in that identity for life, stripping them of agency, re-enforcing a sense of inescapable helplessness that keeps them pinned down, when the truth is, if they stopped looking for excuses as to why they can't do something, and stopped playing the victim, and stopped viewing the world through the Intersectional lens, they would discover they are capable of more than they realised and many of the perceived barriers don't even exist. It doesn't do well to encourage people to feel victimised. Far better to push them towards achievement, with all the struggle and character development that would entail.

8
DIVISION

The next obvious problem with Intersectional Theory is that it causes needless division and hatred between people who should really have no quarrel. As we established earlier, according to this theory, for every victim, there must be a villain. For everyone who is oppressed, there must be an oppressor. And therefore, it pits people against one another for the wholly spurious reasons we have already explained. Whether it be across lines of sex, race, or anything else, this division is damaging to everyone involved.

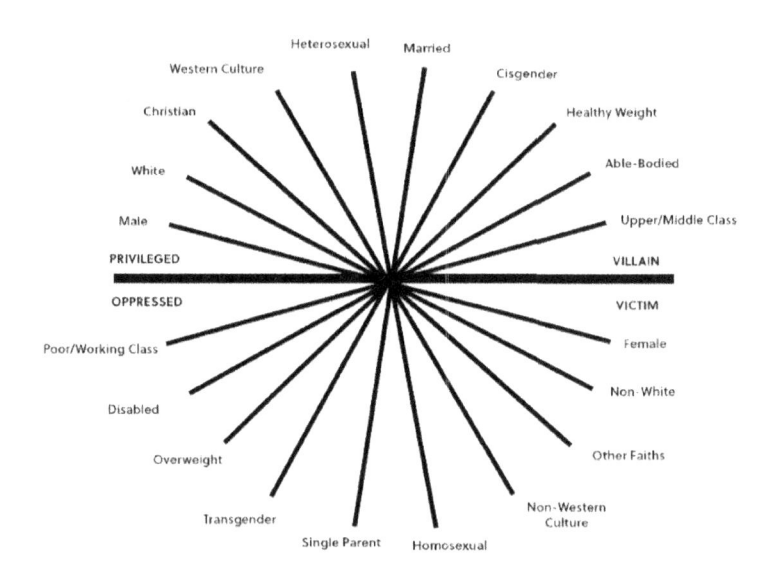

Division Between The Sexes

For example, Intersectional Theory has pitted women against men and taught women that men are toxic oppressors. Through this framework, far from being complementary protectors and providers who are designed to bless women, as outlined in the Bible, men are now portrayed as the enemies of women. Patriarchy is seen as a root of all evil. And as I mentioned briefly before, this has fuelled a wave of feminist hatred against men culminating in trending hashtags on Twitter/X such as #menaretrash and #killallmen.

In the event that not all men can be killed, the Woke have decided that men must simply evolve to become more like women. I referred to this piece in "Trench" but it's worth briefly repeating here. A Huffington Post article written by a half Egyptian feminist writer called Salma Ed-Wardany in 2018 says, "If you listen carefully on any given day, you'll hear the words 'men are trash' like a gentle hum vibrating across the globe. An anthem if you will. A call to arms and a battle cry. A sign of solidarity even. Enter any room, social event, dinner party, creative gathering and you'll hear the phrase from at least one corner of the room, and you'll naturally gravitate towards that group of women because you immediately know you've found your tribe…The phrase, 'men are trash' can actually directly be translated into; 'masculinity is in transition and it's not moving f****** fast enough…So when women across the land cry out, 'men are trash', what it really means is, your ideas of manhood are no longer fit for purpose and your lack of evolution is hurting us all."[1] The "evolution" she means is that men need to put away their inherent "toxic" masculinity and become more like women.

Men, for their part, have felt this hatred and rejection and are increasingly backing away from women who have imbibed Intersectional Theory. Realising that men can now be professionally destroyed for sexual harassment if he looks at a woman for more than five seconds or asks her out on a date twice, like Stephen Henderson experienced, and realising women are increasingly infected with ideas that are hostile towards masculinity, men seem to have largely decided such women are now undesirable for relationships and no longer worth the effort or risk.

A recent survey by Pew discovered that around 63% of men under 30 are now single, choosing to remain unattached.[2] In recent years, we've seen many of them joining wife-renouncing movements like "Men Going Their Own Way (MGTOW)" and the rise of what's been called, "Sigma Males." This is essentially a subculture of men who, instead of pursuing women for marriage, have decided to live a life of self-reliance, redirecting their energies towards self-improvement and financial success. They revel in their independence and in their status as a "lone wolf."

Other men who really do still want to get married, have often decided that since Wokeness is typically a Western phenomenon, they may still be able to find women uninfected by Intersectionality overseas. Called, "Passport Bros," they are defined in Urban Dictionary as, "men who have chosen to seek out foreign women from other countries for relationships. They believe that Western women have been influenced by cultural and societal pressures to behave in a certain way (Intersectional Theory), and that by seeking out foreign women, they can find a more authentic, fulfilling, and harmonious relationship."[3] It's also defined in the same place as, "Men...who choose to live in countries where their money goes further and they're treated with more respect, particularly by women. Passport Bros understand that their lives would be better in places like Southeast Asia and Eastern Europe because strong family values are still seen as the norm in places like that. Hook-up culture isn't as rampant in those parts of the world, and thus the population, especially the women, are far less damaged."[3]

The description is telling. Men are often viewing women who are filled with Intersectional Theory as damaged goods, and are simply doing everything they can to escape them. It's not too hard to see why. When women who believe in it have been taught to hate men as toxic oppressors merely for being men, it can only lead to less harmonious relationships. Men have decided they don't want to marry people who hate them. It means that marriage rates in the West are now at their lowest level since records began in 1862. According to reports in 2022, there are now only 18 marriages per 1,000 unmarried men, and 17 marriages per 1,000 unmarried women.[4] Since 1972, marriage rates have fallen by about 50%.

None of this is indicative of a healthy society and enmity between men and women doesn't help either sex to thrive. Indeed, in the battle of the sexes, both sides lose. As the Bible clearly outlines, men and women were designed for one another, to complement one another, and to be a blessing to one another. Both sexes have been given unique strengths and when given for the good of the other, it causes each sex to flourish. Men are to be a source of love, protection and provision for women. Women are to be a source of love, support and respect for men. When the two come together in harmonious marriage—both sacrificing of themselves for the other—they build strong nuclear families, and raise healthy, happy children. This, in turn, is the foundation of a strong, prosperous, happy society. When that mutual love between the sexes is broken, and when it's replaced by suspicion and hatred, it not only leads to more individual pain and loneliness, but it causes a weakening of the social fabric of society. That's what pervasive Intersectionality has done in recent years.

Racial Division

Intersectionality has also pitted various ethnic minorities against each other too—especially against white people—often with no justification. As we saw earlier through the example of Aruna Khilanani, we now have Woke lecturers in some of the most respected universities in the world fantasising aloud about putting bullets in white people's heads and placing them in shallow graves for no other reason than the colour of their skin. Edinburgh University has conducted a seminary called, "Whiteness. A problem for our time."[5] The University of Chicago announced in 2022 that it would be running an entire course called, "The Problem of Whiteness."[6] A quick Google search for "whiteness" reveals a myriad of blogs ruminating on "The Problem With White People,"[7] and "The Whiteness Problem."[8] In these places, the Woke speak openly and with a sense of virtue about how they might tear down white people, make the world less white, and even create a world without any white people in it. Harvard Magazine published an article in 2022 entitled, "Abolish The White Race."[9] One of the celebrated originators of this idea, called Noel Ignatiev, writes, "The point is not to interpret Whiteness but to abolish it."[10] Elsewhere, a Pakistani writer called Mohsin Hamid, received acclaim from the Woke for a novel he wrote called "The Last White Man." In it, he gave "a glimpse of a future without white people."[11] In 2016, a professor at Philadelphia college tweeted, "All I want for Christmas is White Genocide."[12] He then followed it up by saying, "To clarify: when the whites were massacred during the Haitian Revolution, that was a good thing indeed."

As I mentioned earlier in this book, stoking the idea that one particular race is the root of all the world's problems and suggesting that if they could only be eradicated a utopia would emerge, is a very dangerous idea, and is exactly what the Nazis were teaching in the late 1930s. The target of the race-hatred may be different this time around, but the sentiments are exactly the same: "That particular race is inherently evil. It would be better for all of us if they were eliminated." How can such genocidal sentiments lead to anything good? How can it not do anything but cause needless division? Let's hope Intersectionality doesn't inspire history to repeat itself, but the fact people are feeling emboldened to say these things at all, and in some of the most venerable institutions in the Western hemisphere, tells us how deeply rooted this hateful ideology has become.

If nothing else, Intersectionality has set race relations back several decades. Ever since Martin Luther King Jr.'s famous "I Have A Dream Speech" in 1963, Western society had been gradually working itself towards a "colour-blind" future. There was a growing understanding that if we wanted to create an harmonious society, we would need to start looking beyond such superficial things as skin-colour, and instead treat one another as fellow human beings, each one made in God's own image—no real difference between any of us—and nothing that should matter so much as the content of our character. That attitude was working. Over the second half of the 20th Century, racism had clearly been declining. People increasingly began to no longer care about the triviality of skin colour.

And then Intersectionality arrived. This hateful ideology told people not only to see skin colour, but to see nothing *but* colour, and to make it the most important and defining thing about any person. The same theory then pitted the races against one another and taught non-whites to hate whites, portraying them as villainous monsters who were out to oppress. Because of this, there is now unnecessary suspicion and division between the races again…to the extent that there has even been the reintroduction of race segregation and "black-only" spaces. In 2018, the official City of Cambridge website in Massachusetts published an article called, "Why People of Color Need Spaces Without White People."[13] There, it was argued that the mere presence of white people leads to oppression and unsafety. In Paris in 2017, there was a feminist Intersectional festival that created black-only spaces, and it was roundly celebrated by the left-wing media.[14] In December 2023, BBC Radio 5 Live presenter, Nihal Arthanayke said the "overwhelmingly white" working environment was bad for his mental health. He said, "It's really affecting me that I walk in and all I see is white people."[15]

Obviously division over race is never good for society, as history will attest, but this is another thing that Intersectionality has done to us. There is now quarrel between people who should have no quarrel, and it's happening for the most arbitrary of reasons—including the shade of our skin.

9
PARANOIA

I recently heard a story of an experiment called the Dartmouth Scar Experiment. As the name suggests, it was conducted at Dartmouth College in New Hampshire, and it involved make-up artists painting scars onto the faces of 27 male and 21 female participants. After the scars had been drawn, they showed the participants what they now looked like with a pocket mirror so they could get used to their new identities, and it was explained to them that they were now going to leave the room and interact with people in the building. The researchers explained that they wanted to find out if people discriminated against them, or behaved differently towards them in any way, now that they had facial disfigurements.

Before they left the room however, the make-up artists told the participants that the scars needed some final touch-ups. But what the make-up artist actually did was remove the scars entirely. Participants left the room believing they had a scar on their face when they didn't. When they reported back with their experiences however, they overwhelmingly said that people stared at their scars; that they had been victimised during the day; and that people had generally been mean and rude to them. Some participants even reported how they felt some people had actually subtly referenced the scars on their faces during conversations.[1]

What the experiment proved is that when you tell people that they are victims because of things and suggest others might treat them differently because of it, like for example, their sex or the colour of their skin, they will become primed to see sexism, racism and general discrimination everywhere…even when it doesn't really exist. Filling people's heads with Intersectional Theory has done this to our society. We now have a population that is paranoid they're being discriminated against every day when they're not; who have been encouraged to take offence when none was intended; and to see non-existent sexism and racism around every corner. This is causing people to behave uncharitably towards one another, and to believe the worst about one another's intentions.

There's a story the Scottish comedian, Billy Connolly, once told of the time his sister was on a bus in Glasgow. He says that when she got onto the bus, "she sat down and it just so happened to be the last seat. And the bus trundled off into the day. Four or five stops later, the bus stops and a wee dwarf woman comes on…she discovered there was no seat and so hung onto whatever was nearest—the seat or pole or whatever. And so the bus took off. Now there was a wee schoolgirl in her school uniform sitting over here. Probably urged along by her mother…she went over to the wee dwarf woman and she said, "excuse me. Would you like to have my seat?" Whereupon the wee dwarf woman flew into a rage. "Oh aye! Because I'm a dwarf?! You're offering me a seat simply because I'm a dwarf! Well, I have managed my whole life as a dwarf. It's not a problem to me! Keep your seat!" The girl, cringing with embarrassment went back to her seat and the bus trundled on in silent embarrassment for a stop or three.

Then a big Glasgow woman was getting off the bus. But before she went up to the door she went over to the wee dwarf woman. She tapped her on the shoulder and said, "I'm getting off the bus and I'm leaving my empty seat here." The dwarf interjected, "Because I'm a dwarf?!"

"No!" said the big Glasgow woman. "Not because you're a dwarf but because you're another human being. I happen to be leaving the bus. My seat is vacant. I'm merely pointing it out to you that it exists. As a matter of fact, I thought you were extremely rude to that wee girl and you owe her an apology. As a matter of fact, I hope when you go home tonight, Snow White kicks your [butt]."[2]

The dwarf woman had been so primed to see herself as a victim and was so self-conscious, that she had become paranoid and uncharitable about the motives of others. Rather than believing the best in humanity, she had had come to see discrimination in every interaction, and was taking offence when none was intended. When the schoolgirl offered her seat, she no longer saw it as a basic act of courtesy for another human being as she should have, but an act of condescension.

With the spread of Intersectional Theory, similar good deeds are now going punished every day, all over the Western world. Men are holding doors open for women and instead of being thanked for a courteous act, are being chastised for "misogyny." A man who tries to explain something to a woman will now not be thanked for taking the time to impart his knowledge, but will instead be accused of "mansplaining." This is where women are encouraged to feel that in the act of a man merely conveying information, he is somehow condescending her and she should take offence for it.

What do we think the result of this endless paranoia is? The result is that people stop offering their seats to others on the bus; men stop holding doors open for women or trying to help them with information even when they could give it. Referring back to earlier examples, it's a world where men will now refuse to ask a woman out, even when he likes her, and it's a world where he won't make eye-contact for longer than five seconds. And consequently, because of all this paranoia and uncharitable behaviour, the world becomes a less friendly, less warm place to be. We all suffer by it.

Race Paranoia

As for race paranoia, Intersectional Theory has produced a lot of that as well. In 2021 the BBC reported how 98% of the English countryside population was white, so sought out some of the 2% who were not white to suggest to them they may have been the victims of racism. They found Jag Patel, of Asian descent, who opened a newspaper shop in rural Gillingham and upon thinking about it, agreed saying, "What's difficult is when people come into the shop and they quite clearly have a 'face' at you."[3] Now does someone having a face on them necessarily mean they're racist? Could it not also be because they've had a bad day? Or because they've had argument with their spouse? Or they don't like the weather? Or maybe that's just their face! Exposure to Intersectionality however, primes people to see racism everywhere.

Criminologist and co-author of Rural Racism, Professor Neil Chakraborty has also decided that 'face' is probably 'covert racism.' He says, "victims are often left unsure if what they are experiencing is discrimination. Being made to wait for food to be served in a restaurant or café, or sometimes even complete refusal—you feel uncomfortable describing this as racism because you're thinking, 'Is this me? Am I being too demanding?' Noticing people were crossing the street to avoid you. Why is this happening? Is it me? Am I intimidating? Persistent staring…"

Let's be fair…we've all been made to wait for food at a restaurant—that's a universal experience. As is being told they are fully booked and have no tables available. Professor Chakraborty, however, has been primed to suspect that whenever it happens to him it has something to do with the colour of his skin. Ditto, if someone happens to be crossing the road up ahead, or looks at him for too long. Intersectionality has made people paranoid about the nature of the people around them, and rather than seeing the best in them, has encouraged people to see the worst. Again, this is obviously not healthy for the cohesion of social fabric and doesn't make for friendly communities. Priming people to see discrimination everywhere has made the world colder and more unforgiving.

10
UNCHARITABLE

What exacerbates the situation is that it actually now pays if you can prove your neighbour was being misogynistic or racist. By besmirching their good name, and basically destroying the lives of others, you can fast-track yourself to status and glory. This is causing an increase of the uncharitable behaviour.

To be Uncharitable Pays

I was twelve-years-old when I visited the United States for the first time, and in those days—far more than today—there were significant cultural differences compared to the United Kingdom that I and my family found fascinating.

Most of these differences I enjoyed. For example, I loved the bonhomie of service staff in the United States who would always greet you far more enthusiastically than at home, and upon your departure would be sure to wish you, "have a nice day." I loved the portion sizes of the food which were bigger than at home and that for example, if you ordered a pancake in a restaurant, rather than just one, you'd get a stack as big as your head. There was a lot to enjoy about American culture.

One of the less appealing things that I remember my parents, and especially my dad, being bemused about however, was the litigation culture in the US. My dad was a policeman so this was an area of particular interest to him—hence why he was also obsessed with the show, COPS and would watch it every evening. I remember while watching the ad breaks on American TV, how local lawyers would frequently pop on screen to encourage viewers to think of ways in which they may have been wronged in the recent past, because if they could identify one, there was a chance this firm would be able to sue on their behalf and make some money out of it.

Perhaps they'd tripped on a kerb and hurt their knee? Perhaps they'd pet a cat on the street and it had scratched them? Perhaps they'd been using a vacuum cleaner and tripped over the cord and injured themselves? Perhaps they'd drunk a hot coffee from a vendor and burned their tongue? Perhaps they'd closed a kitchen drawer and jammed their finger? Perhaps they'd been on a rollercoaster and been sick? Think! Think of something!

In the UK in those days, these kinds of incidents were considered accidents—a part of the risk of living. Nobody would dream of suing over such things. If you tripped on a kerb and fell, they would accept it was their own fault for not looking where they were going. If you went to pet a cat of unknown temperament, you'd accept the risk it may take a sudden dislike to you and have a swipe. If you tripped over a vacuum cleaner cord, again that's on you. If your tongue got burned on hot coffee from a vendor, you should have tested the temperature before having a glug. If you jammed your finger in the drawer, that's your fault too. Getting sick on a rollercoaster is just one of the known potential hazards of rollercoasters. This is how we thought in the United Kingdom in those days. Accept responsibility for your own accidents and don't try to blame anyone else for them.

When we arrived in the United States though, we found a very different notion. In the US, "if there was pain, there was a claim." If you had hurt yourself or been the victim of any kind of pain, there was normally going to be someone you could blame for that, and along with it, there was likely money to be made. That kerb trip? That's not your own fault. No, no, no. That's the local government's fault for putting that kerb there and not painting it a bright colour to alert you to its existence. Did you pet a cantankerous cat that lashed out? You could sue the cat owner for letting the dangerous creature out. Did you trip over the vacuum cord? You could go after the manufacturers and say they should have made the cord a brighter colour so it could be more easily seen. Did you burn your tongue on hot coffee? You could sue the vendor for making it too hot and not putting enough warning labels on it. Did you jam your fingers? You could sue the cabinet makers saying they should have in-built safety features to prevent it. Did you barf on a rollercoaster? You could sue the park operator for your distress, saying there should have been more warning signs about the violent nature of the ride.

The problem seemed to be that these claims were often successful. They should have been thrown out but they weren't. If you could find a way to pin the blame on someone else, you *could* indeed make some money. Often quite a lot of money. The thing that bothered my dad most about this litigation culture—and as I've grown up I've come to see it now myself, especially as it has spread to the UK and we now get the same adverts—is that it encourages people to be vindictive towards one another. By that I mean, deliberately malicious, cruel, merciless, vengeful, unforgiving, retaliatory, and ruthless. Rather than accepting with good humour that accidents sometimes happen and writing them off as part of daily life; rather than admitting we are largely responsible for the ones we experience; and rather than looking charitably upon others who were simply doing their best to provide us with goods or a service, and who couldn't have possibly anticipated the problems you would encounter, it encourages people to vindictively impoverish others for their own benefit.

Intersectionality has encouraged a similar kind of vindictiveness in our culture. If you can make a convincing claim that you've been the victim of misogyny or racism, there are quite big prizes to be won. If that dwarf woman on the Glasgow bus complained loud enough about discrimination, she could probably have won a payout from the bus company for not dealing with the situation, or perhaps from the little schoolgirl's family. Almost certainly she could have gotten something out of the big woman who made the joke about Snow White as well. If a woman can convince her company that she was condescended by a man who held a door open or "mansplained" something to her, and that she felt distressed because he looked at her for more than five seconds, she could probably win a payout from that company. The man would likely be fired and have his life ruined, but she would get her payout.

Likewise, if Mr Patel of Gillingham could identify the customer(s) who supposedly made a 'face' in his store and were to make a complaint of racism, there would probably be a financial reward for him there too. Reputational and professional destruction for the other guy(s). But a financial reward and high status for him. If Professor Chakraborty complained of racism because of having to wait for food in a restaurant, he could probably get financial compensation from that restaurant. Workers in the restaurant might lose their jobs and the restaurant itself might have its name dragged through the mud and be forced to close…but Professor Chakraborty would get his payout.

We're seeing a lot of this kind of thing today then. People who, being determined to portray themselves as victims so that they might reap the rewards, are behaving uncharitably towards others. Even being willing to destroy their reputations, livelihoods and lives in the process. Remember, for every victim, there must be a villain. For every oppression, there must be an oppressor. Therefore, every time someone is determined to portray themselves as a victim, there's usually someone else—often an innocent—who is paying the price. Remember how I earlier mentioned the brief craze of women deliberately working out in revealing gym gear, then recording it on their phones, in the hope they can catch a man looking in their general direction and who could therefore be accused of sexual harassment? In winning herself the social media status, she conceivably ends up ruining a man's life. But that's the kind of world Intersectional Theory is creating. It's becoming a dog-eat-dog kind of world where in order to raise yourself up, someone else has to be dragged down. For every time you want to portray yourself as oppressed, you have to find someone who gets destroyed as your oppressor. Often these "oppressors" are no such thing.

Jordan Peterson recently spoke about something like this with podcaster Chris Williamson. While working for the New York Times, a journalist called Nellie Bowles wrote a hit piece on Peterson, which he described as being personally "devastating." Three years later, after Bowles had left the newspaper, she wrote another piece where she opened up on the culture that existed there. She said, "the game was to devastate someone else's reputation in the attempt to boost yours."[1] That's a great way of describing what's happened in our culture through Intersectionality. We are now a society filled with people who are desperate to destroy other's reputations because by doing so they can boost their own.

11
TURNING GOOD INTO EVIL

Having outlined some of the general problems that Intersectional Theory is creating for society, we're next going to go around the matrix looking at each of the points of division in turn.

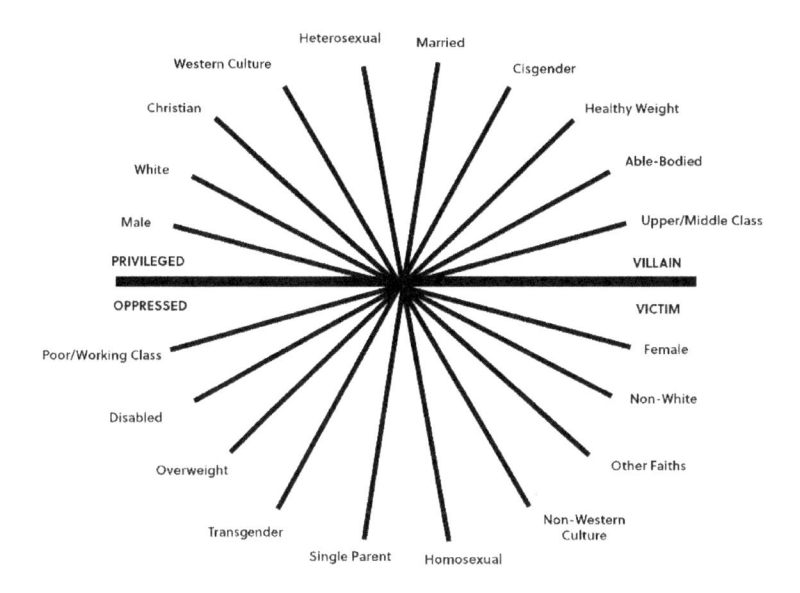

```
                    Heterosexual   Married
          Western Culture              Cisgender
          Christian                         Healthy Weight
        White                                    Able-Bodied
       Male                                        Upper/Middle Class
       PRIVILEGED                                  VILLAIN
       ━━━━━━━━━━━━━━━━━━━━━━━━━━━━━━━━━━━━━━━━
       OPPRESSED                                   VICTIM
       Poor/Working Class                        Female
                                                Non-White
         Disabled
            Overweight                        Other Faiths
                                            Non-Western
                   Transgender                Culture
                     Single Parent  Homosexual
```

I think what will become clear is that when you tear down everything *above* the horizontal line, you will tear down much that is good. Similarly, when you celebrate or raise up everything *below* the horizontal line, you will raise up much that is evil. Indeed, through this framework, good often becomes evil, and evil becomes good. That's why this book is called "The Woke Inversion." This matrix literally inverts right and wrong. And "What sorrow for those who say that evil is good and good is evil, that dark is light and light is dark, that bitter is sweet and sweet is bitter." (Isaiah 5:20)

SECTION 2

SPECIFIC PROBLEMS

12
WHAT MEN DO

Let's start with the male and female division. According to Intersectional Theory, maleness is something to be torn down while femaleness is only something to be raised up.

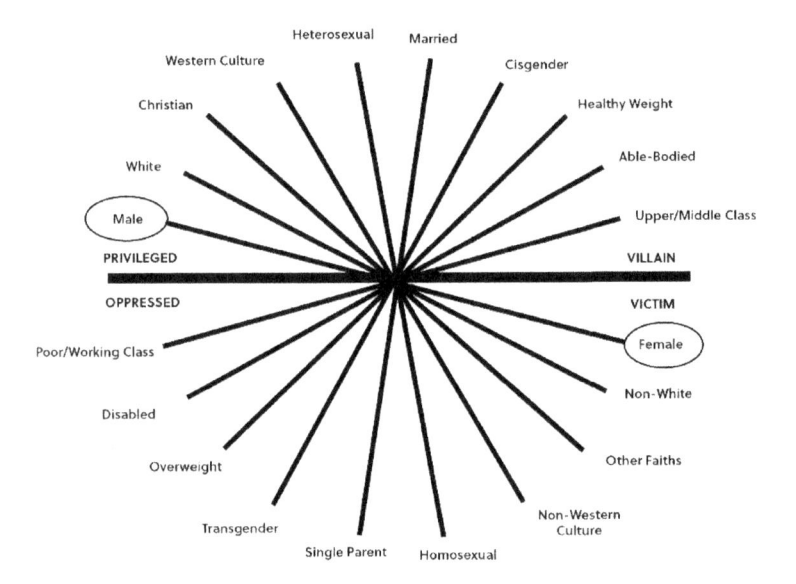

As we have already noted, the application of the theory means men are increasingly under attack in the Woke world of Postmodernity. They are told they are inherently trash and should be killed; that the world would be better off without them; that their masculinity is neither wanted or needed; and that they need to reform themselves to become more like women. Because I'm researching for this book, YouTube is currently recommending to me a lot of videos around this theme. Recently, I watched some street interviews in the United States where the question being posed to random citizens was, "Are men trash?" One pink-haired feminist had no hesitation in excitedly pronouncing, "Oh! Cis, heterosexual men, absolutely! Especially white men."[1]

These constant attacks are clearly beginning to have an effect on male well-being. Just this morning, I watched another recommended video on YouTube by the channel, "Baggage Claim." If you're unfamiliar with this channel, it's by an American woman of Asian descent who critiques Western culture and who specifically exposes the negative effects Intersectionality has had in the world of entertainment. In this video, she was talking about how lately, Hollywood has consistently released material that demeans, emasculates and belittles men, and how there are real statistics to show men are now collectively struggling pretty hard with things like loneliness, depression, and suicide. She then showed an array of comments from people who were responding to this information. There was not much sympathy to say the least. One wrote, "Male loneliness is not real and not valid." Another said, "Men are lonely because they are terrible people." Another, "Why tf should anyone have empathy for men?" Another said, "men are subhuman." Another, "most men are born useless and are meant to die alone." Another wrote, "nah male suicide rate needa be higher actually." Another declared, "Men are misogynistic demons." Another, "You don't understand the pleasure it gives me to see these men crying and depressed."[2]

Although Intersectionality has taught the Woke that vitriolic hatred of men is justified and puts them on the right side of history, of course it is fatally misguided. The world needs men of all shades and colours, and it needs their masculinity.

What Men Do

Men don't get a lot of thanks for it—indeed, it seems their efforts barely get noticed at all—but they do a lot of good for our society. Because of their natural strength, imagination, playfulness, adventurous spirit, industriousness, and their desire to build, they have created the infrastructure of the world as we know it today.

We have cars because of men. Karl Benz—a man—is widely recognised to have invented the automobile. It was a man, a Scottish chemist called James Young, who figured out we could run them on something called gasoline. It was Young who also saw the wider potential of oil, which now lubricates almost every piece of machinery you can think of. It was men that figured out you could use the leftover oil to do a whole lot more. Just a few petroleum based products invented by men include nylon and polyester clothing, insect repellents, dentures, umbrellas, shampoos, hair colouring, lipstick, eye-glasses, telephones, cameras, pillows, dishes, rope, parachutes, toothpaste, guitar strings, bandages, artificial limbs, folding doors and much more.[3] A British engineer called Richard Trevithick invented the train. The Wright Brothers invented the plane. Benjamin Franklin, Alessandro Volta and Michael Faraday discovered usable electricity. Thomas Edison, Joseph Swan and Hiram Maxim then used it to create the first light-bulbs. Alexander Graham-Bell made the telephone. John Logie Baird made the television. Hubert Cecil Booth and Daniel Hess created the vacuum cleaner. Charles Babbage invented the computer. Tim Berners-Lee gave us the internet. Adam Smith created the monetary system; John Napier the decimal system; Alexander Cummings the flushing toilet; Kirkpatrick MacMillan the bicycle;

Joseph Niepce the camera; James Maxwell the colour photograph; Alexander Wood the hypodermic syringe; Alexander Fleming penicillin; Robert Watson-Watt the microwave and radar; John Dunlop the pneumatic tyre; John McAdam tarmac roads; William Cullen refrigeration; William LeBaron Jenny the skyscraper; and Albert Einstein the Theory of General Relativity. If nothing else, feminists should be thankful to Earl Haas—a man—who invented the modern tampon applicator. Most of them are also in debt to Luis Miramontes, Gregory Goodwin Pincus and Carl Djerassi, who invented the contraceptive pill.

The house you live in, and almost every building you see around you, was likely designed and built by men. Often at least partly with their bare hands. As of 2022, 95.83% of people working in construction are men and 95.78% of design and development engineers are men.[4] 96.31% of floorers and tilers are men. 96.47% of glaziers are men. 96.6% of plasterers are men. Your house was probably painted by a man too, given that 94.98% of painters and decorators are men. Most of the furniture inside will also come from men since they make up 85.98% of furniture makers and craft woodworkers. Men are probably responsible for keeping your immediate surroundings tidy as well. 90.35% of gardeners and landscapers are men. 90.47% of groundsmen and park keepers are men. If you want to look out your window to admire that garden or park, you can likely see it clearly because of men, given that 91.81% of window cleaners are men.

If the lights, heating and appliances in your home actually work on a day-to-day basis, in the sense they stay powered, it's usually men who are to be thanked. Men are typically the ones who mine most of the coal we burn for energy—96.2% of miners are men. They are also the ones who typically work on oil rigs or in refineries—95% of them are men. Enrico Fermi—a man—was the first to develop a functioning nuclear power station and it's typically men who build and maintain them too. Even in the so-called green economy, although I didn't find any specific figures for this, because of their prevalence in the field of engineering, it's likely that men installed the wind generators or solar panels that serve your home.

If anything in your house goes wrong, it's overwhelmingly likely that a man that will come to fix it. 98.27% of electricians are men. 98.05% of plumbers are men. 98.97% of carpenters and joiners are men. If the car on your driveway breaks down, a man will almost certainly fix that too given that 99.19% of vehicle technicians, mechanics and electricians are men. The car parts required to make the repairs were probably delivered by a man as well—92.65% of van drivers are men. 97.36% of fork-lift drivers are men. 97.34% of large goods vehicles are driven by men. Men are generally the ones responsible for moving things around the country and getting them where they need to be.

If you want to transport yourself somewhere, you're probably going to rely on a man for that too. 92% of bus and coach drivers are men, 91.91% of train drivers are men, and 90.7% of aircraft pilots and engineers are men. 84.95% of air traffic controllers are men too.

If you ate food today, it was likely only possible because of men. 82.07% of farmers in England are men, and in Scotland it's 93%. 90.5% of the butchers are men. Even if you ate out in a restaurant rather than at home, 79.13% of the chefs are men. And again, the heavy goods vehicles that get the food from depots to supermarkets and restaurants were probably driven by men.

If you get into trouble pretty much anywhere, and need some form of rescuing, it's likely a man that's going to do it. In 2023, in the

United States, 86.7% of full-time law enforcement officers were male.[5] 95.6% of firefighters were men.[6] If you need to be rescued in the ocean off the coast of the United Kingdom, there are 4,600 volunteers working for the Royal National Lifeboat Association (RNLI) and only 300 are women, so there's a 93.48% chance it'll be a man that comes to your aid.[7] I couldn't find figures for mountain rescues but I believe they would be similar. As we saw earlier, men also make up the large majority of those employed by the armed forces (84.3%), meaning it's men who are largely keeping our country safe at home and abroad, especially on the front-line. They'll also be the ones to shovel snow from sidewalks and put down sandbags in the case of floods.

We could continue but I think the point has been made. Are men, as the Woke insist, really trash? Are they really good for ***nothing***? Should they all be killed? Does the world really not need their strength or masculinity? Is it really toxic? Are they really inherently terrible people? Are they, as one commenter said, subhuman? Can we really read these statistics and fairly reach the conclusion that they are born useless and deserve to die alone? Are they not deserving of empathy when they begin to struggle? Should they really commit suicide in higher numbers? Are they really deserving of such venomous vitriol simply for being men? Are they not deserving of at least some acknowledgement and gratitude for the ways in which they have endeavoured to make our lives better, and for the ways in which they daily give of themselves so that we can eat, work and live in a functioning society of relative comfort? If men downed their tools even for one day, the world would quickly begin to fall apart. Nobody would really want a world without them. It's only the facile nature of Intersectionality that makes anyone think they would.

Could Women Do It Too?

Woke ideologues would give an angry retort to these statistics. According to Intersectional Theory, it's impossible that men could ever do anything with positive intentions. No. The only reason men dominate in these jobs is, they say, because women just aren't given the opportunities to do them as well. Men are subjugating women under a tyrannically patriarchal system that forces them to stay out of the sphere of Science, Technology, Engineering and Mathematics (STEM) and that instead chains them at home to the kitchen stove, where they are forced to raise children, sew and make soup. Women, the Woke say, would love to be out in the rain laying sewage pipes, or under the ground mining coal, or under cars getting covered in grease, but it's the system! The system keeps them down! They refuse to believe what seems to be obvious to the rest of us—that men and women are simply different. They each have different strengths and different interests. The reason there's such huge disparity in the numbers of men and women doing these jobs is simply because men are inherently drawn to them in a way that women aren't. Women aren't involved in a lot of these jobs, not because they're being oppressed or held down by a misogynistic system, but because they just don't **want** to be. They don't *really* want to be laying sewage pipes in the rain or fixing cars all day or working down coal mines. Not in general. Not the same extent as men do. In the main, they like that men exist to do these things for them. It's like that old meme of a woman looking out the window saying, "it's time to fight for gender equality!" She then realises it's been snowing outside overnight and it will need to be shovelled from the driveway. "Better wait until Spring," she decides.

This is ok, by the way! Good men don't mind getting out in the cold and shovelling snow. I dare say there's a part of them that even enjoys it. But what they do mind, is their efforts going completely unnoticed, and instead of being thanked for bringing their masculinity to bear, being told it makes them toxic trash, and that they're good for nothing, and that they deserve to die.

Even though we live in an age of true female emancipation where there is absolutely nothing stopping women getting involved in STEM jobs at all, and even though there are heavily targeted campaigns trying to convince them that this is where their future lies, they still only make up 35% of the STEM students.[8] In areas such as Computer Science and Engineering, they only make up 19%. Women simply aren't as interested in some of these career paths. And again, that's ok. Why should they be forced if it's not a natural interest? Women have their own natural strengths and interests—things where men need them in equal measure.

Expedite Robinson

I've spoken about this in previous series but it bears repeating. There's a survival show on Dutch television called "Expedite Robinson." In one early season of this show, they placed a group of men on a desert island, and a group of women on another. Both sexes were given nothing, and the idea was to see how each one would set about building a civilisation on their respective patches of land.

The male island developed well. They immediately started building infrastructure to make it a more comfortable place to live. They constructed huts to live in using locally sourced materials. They created sleeping areas, built dining tables, sanitation solutions, established a system for catching fish, a cooking rota, and very quickly had a proper, functioning civilisation. They seemed to be absolutely loving it as well. They were seen constantly joking and having fun as they happily beavered away with their construction projects.

The women's island, in contrast, didn't develop at all. There seemed to be no natural instinct to build some infrastructure. They didn't construct shelters; they didn't build tables to eat on; they didn't build beds or come up with sanitation solutions. Their camp remained something of a mess. Furthermore, they descended into bickering. No woman was able to command the authority of the group. Any time someone tried to take a lead role, they just squabbled, complained, fought over personal possessions and got nowhere. There was a lot of tears and stress in the women's camp.

When it was time to mix up the sexes, and for each side to see the camp belonging to the other gender, the women were confused at how advanced and orderly the male island was. Popular culture had conditioned them to believe that men were useless buffoons. One woman commented "I thought I had arrived on a dream island. I'm in heaven. It's like a beach café." Another said, "You would think that at the women's camp, everything would be orderly, but compared to this it was pure chaos at our place. Here, everything is orderly and neat."[9]

The men were equally confused by the lack of development on the female island, but upon arrival, they instinctively set about making it habitable. Soon, both islands were brought up to speed. This led one of the women to remark, "I once read an interview with a social biologist who said that if the world was only women, we would still be living in the stone age. After this, I believe it." The quote was actually from Camille Paglia who wrote, "If civilization had been left in female hands, we would still be living in grass huts."[10]

There have been other survival shows throughout the years where the results of Expedite Robinson have been replicated. Bear Grylls, for example, made a show for Channel 4 in the UK called The Island and upon the same premise, the exact same things happened. While the women began with confidence boldly declaring, "we don't need men!" they soon discovered otherwise. The women didn't know how to build shelters, or hunt for food, or attain clean water, and thus became so dangerously dehydrated that they began to faint and suffer from malnutrition. Through tears and exhaustion they admitted that all they really wanted to do was go home. The men, on the other hand, were again seen having the time of their lives, cheering and high-fiving one another as they caught fish and snakes to eat, made stews, built fires to keep warm, and huts to sleep in and stay dry.[11] Quite simply, men have instincts and strengths that women don't have. It shouldn't be controversial to say it. And if we didn't have men being men, society would never have even got started. If men stopped being men for just a day, the infrastructure of the world would fall apart. To hate them, as Intersectionality encourages, is to hate a really good thing. More than that, it's to hate a really necessary thing. Tearing men down and deriding masculinity as toxic is only going to harm our society.

13
WHAT WOMEN DO

Intersectional Theory is not only abusive towards men, but in a slightly different, yet no less destructive way, it's abusive to women as well. By teaching women, that by sheer virtue of their sex, they are inherently inferior to men—an oppressed victim from birth—they are stripped of agency and taught that their femininity is a weakness. Something to be cast off. Indeed, the underlying message of Intersectional Theory is that to be equal with men, women must become *like* men.

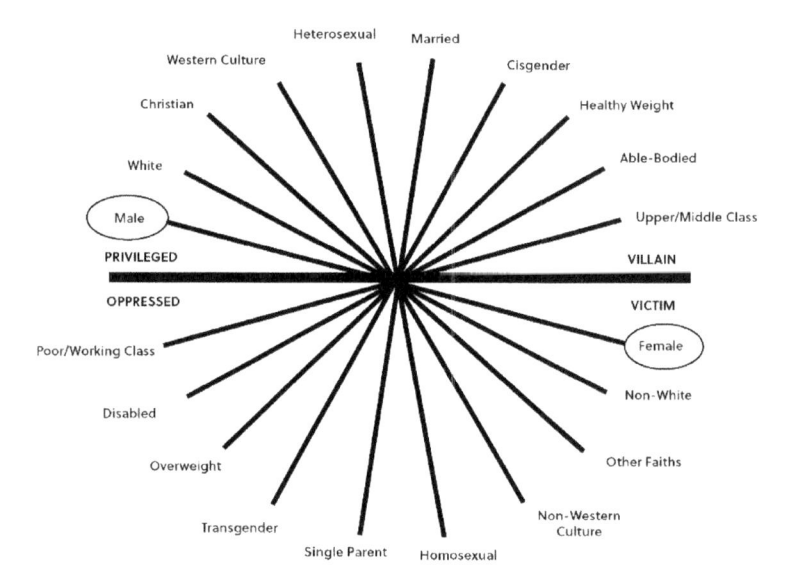

That's what Intersectionality teaches. That in order to create equality and level the playing field, men must be dragged down, yes. They must become **disempowered**, yes. But conversely, women must raise themselves up to equality by becoming **empowered** like them. We hear about "female empowerment" all the time these days, but what does that empowerment look like? What does that actually mean? Well in practice, it means they must become more masculine. They must prove that they can do all the things men do, just as well as them, if not better.

An example of where we see this message coming through loud and clear is in the content Hollywood now makes. Since Wokeism became embedded in the entertainment industry, there has been an obsession with putting "strong female characters" on screen who have no feminine traits, but who instead merely mimic men. In recent years, Disney has been particular prominent in this regard. In their Marvel and Star Wars movies in particular, especially those produced in the last 5-10 years, the female characters now show very few traditional feminine traits like empathy, patience, compassion or gentleness. Instead, they are now nearly always depicted as stoic, aggressive, arrogant and immensely strong. Traits traditionally associated with men. Interestingly, these are the same traits that are decried as "toxic" when seen in actual men, but are positively encouraged in women.

It's an abusive message for women—to be told that their femininity makes them innately lesser and that they have to become more manly to achieve equality. And of course, it goes against what we understand as Christians. The Bible is clear that men and women already have equal standing under God. One is not worth more than the other. As it's written, "There is no longer Jew or Gentile, slave or free, male and female. For you are all one in Christ Jesus." (Galatians 3:28) This verse means that both are created in God's image; both are equally invited before the throne of grace; both are equal heirs of God. The Bible acknowledges that men and women have different strengths and weaknesses but declares neither masculinity or femininity is more important than the other. It says, "But among the Lord's people, women are not independent of men, and men are not independent of women." (1 Corinthians 11:11) Each relies on the good things the other naturally provides.

The world needs what men do. But the world needs what women do too. And if women spend their time aiming trying to be men, not only will they be frustrated to find they never get there—women just don't make very good men—but society will then miss out on all the wonderful things femininity naturally offers. The world needs women!

Let Women Be Women

It's been said that while men are more interested in *things*, women are more interested in *people*. Now, we already know men are interested in things. As we saw in the previous chapter, they're fixated on engines, electrical circuits and plumbing. That's why they're always inventing and buildings things and being the ones to keep those things going. But that women are more interested in people should be equally obvious. Because while a man's mind is typically preoccupied with how he's going to build a retaining wall in the backyard, or what his favourite sports team is up to, a woman is far more likely to be preoccupied with people. She's thinking about relationships. How her friend's date went last night. She wants to phone her to get the details. Or even better, arrange to meet for a catch-up. She's wondering if her other friend is doing ok in her marriage. And how they're getting on with the new baby. She's planning a birthday party for Sarah, and wondering when all the girls will be free. Women are simply much more relational. They're better at establishing relationships and keeping those relationships. They're more interested in what people are up to generally. The neighbours. Celebrities, even. These things don't interest the average man to the same extent.

Who is more likely to remember key dates like birthdays and anniversaries? Women. Because they're thinking about it more. Who is more likely to have memorised the ways in which certain people in the community are connected? Women. I don't know how many times a woman has told me a story that went along the lines of, "Remember Donna? Yes, you do. She's the one who's the niece of James, who plays the piano at church? You know James? Yes you do…he's married to Anna? She's the sister of Louise Wilson who lives in London? Louise married Steve Wilson four years ago but they had to move to London last year for his work…." Meanwhile, I genuinely have no idea who any of these people are, and only have a limited interest in finding out. Similarly, who is more likely to get involved in PTA meetings, school plays, amateur dramatics, choirs or community events? Women.

Men don't have this instinct. At least not nearly to the same extent. And it's because they don't have this relational instinct that they often rely on women to make connections for them. Indeed, men who don't have women to create connections for them can begin to struggle with loneliness quite quickly. The comedian, Sebastian Maniscalco, once said that he was like a cat who hides under the bed, and his wife is the one who coaxes him out to be with people every now and then. Jerry Seinfeld, whom he was talking to, agreed, saying that from his observations, wives socialise their husbands. Women are their link to friends and community. And in the same way men actually like shovelling snow for their women, it seems to me that women like making connections for their men. Each likes bringing their strengths to bear for the good of the other.

A few years ago, I was planning to visit Paris—it's only an hour away from where I live and I'd never been, so I decided this was unacceptable and I was going to spend a few days there at long last. I mentioned it to an ex-girlfriend, who is now a friend, who had lived there while at university. I told her about all the ***things*** I was excited to see. The Eiffel Tower. The Louvre. Notre Dame. ***Things***. ***Things*** were what made me excited to visit Paris and I'd filled my schedule with lots of them. My friend wrote back excitedly… "Oh, I can put you in touch with my friends, ____! You can have lunch with them. There's a café nearby, you should meet. I'll write to them to say you're coming. They're a nice couple, they met each other when…" and before long I was being regaled with their life stories. How they met. Their dates. There were many other friends she wanted me to meet as well, giving me the impression that if we'd ended up married and gone together, we would have been spending the majority of the trip meeting people. That's what got her excited. Me? ***Things***. Her? ***People***.

I recognise that I would probably benefit from having someone in my life like that. Indeed, I've got to be honest, although I'm not married, one of the things I'd genuinely be most excited about if I was, would be having someone who remembers when everyone's birthdays are, and who instinctively arranges cards and gifts on behalf of both of us. Women are naturals with that. I, on the other hand, am definitely not and therefore, birthdays and holidays can be a source of tremendous stress!

Even when men do make friendships on their own, they're often just an accidental byproduct of their interest in ***things***. Men's friendships tend to form because they've joined a sports team, or a gym, or a club. Where women's friendships are more intentional, face-to-face, and are fostered through direct communication and support, men's friendships tend to happen side-by-side while coincidentally engaged in a shared activity. For example, men don't tend to make plans to meet one another for a chat, with no other intention than to have deep and meaningful conversations about their personal lives and feelings. No. They merely want to, for example, play golf. That's the goal. Therefore, they call someone who also likes golf so they can play a round. I read a story on Twitter (X) recently that everyone was describing as "peak male friendship." It says, "I have one golf friend I play with regularly. I met him through work and call him Hammer. That might be his last name; I do not know his first name. I called him Kirkland for about a year before he told me he plays Kirkland balls and it's not his name. We don't talk about anything besides golf chit chat. Like, 'your ball is over there, I think it went long' etc. After golf we decide when we are playing the following weekend. I might text him, "golf?" Do I know what he did for Thanksgiving? Nope. Is he married? Kid? I have no idea. I have never done anything besides golf with this guy. We went out 36 times this year. After my dog…BEST FRIEND."[1] The guys just want to golf, the *thing* is the key. Having someone to do it with is just byproduct. And where women will generally be intentional about keeping in *frequent* contact with their friends—making time for each other—guys can go for weeks or months without talking to theirs…if they have any. In 2019, a YouGov study reported that 1 in 5 men had no friends at all. In 2021, the situation appeared to have deteriorated even further. A study by the charity, Movember, discovered a *third* of men in Britain felt they had no close friends, or none at all.[2]

The jobs women naturally aim for tend to be people-focused as well. 84.41% of nurses are women.[3] 94.86% of child-carers are women. 86.69% of nursery and primary teachers are women. 84.79% of beauticians are women. 83.66% of care workers are women. 83.43% of physiotherapists are women. 80.93% of social workers are women. 79.84% of counsellors are women. 89.02% of dancers and choreographers are women. 73.26% of hairdressers and barbers are women. Wherever there's a profession that's focused on people—whether that be caring for them, nurturing them, beautifying them, teaching them or mending their relationships—women will tend to be at the forefront. And that's ok! Just as it's ok for men to prefer STEM jobs. If these are the kind of jobs that women naturally enjoy and gravitate towards, well the world needs them. It seems self-defeating to push women away from the jobs they like and to force them into jobs they don't like—like construction, plumbing, mining and car repair, just to create an arbitrary sense of equality. Let women be women. We need them and their contributions every bit as much as we need men and theirs.

Women Bring Life

Perhaps it's best to think of it like this: Men may build the houses, but it's women who turn them into homes. Men may put up the walls and rooves, but without women to fill them with warmth and life, they remain empty boxes. We haven't even talked about child-bearing, but of course, that is one of their unique gifts—they have the ability to bring forth life. Indeed, the name "Eve," the woman from whom we all descend, literally means "life." That's what women do. They naturally infuse the places they inhabit with life. Not only through child-bearing, but in their natural ability to make connections and build friendships. While men may have built the infrastructure of society, women have traditionally been the ones to turn those towns into communities. The kind of places you'd actually want to live.

Charles Murray, an American Political Scientist, once wrote about how America traditionally ordered its society. He was primarily speaking here about stay-at-home-mums but there's a wider point to be made. He said, "Social Capital is the academic term for the resource that makes American civil society work. It is organised things like teaching English to immigrants or serving on the town council. It is also the guy who shovels snow from the sidewalk of the old lady who lives alone across the street. It is parents at PTA meetings, church-goers organising Christmas plays, candy stripers at the local hospital, and neighbours keeping an eye on each other's houses when no one is home.

The point is that many of the important forms of social capital take more time than a person holding a full-time job can afford. Who has been the primary engine for creating America's social capital throughout its history, making our civil society one of the sociological wonders of the world? People without full-time jobs. The overwhelming majority of those people have been wives.

Every aspect of family and community life gets an infusion of vitality and depth from wives who are not working full-time. If you live in a place that you cherish because "it's a great community," think of the things you have in mind that make it a great community (scenery and restaurants don't count), and then think about who bears the brunt of the load in making those things happen."[4]

It's the women. Women, in the traditional role of homemaker, were the ones who would form bonds with neighbours. But even on a wider scale now that most women work, they will still do this more naturally than men. They'll invite people over for barbecues, bake, get involved in church groups, school events, amateur dramatics, choirs, and turn the bare infrastructure of roads and buildings into a warm place to stay. Now that we're living in an age where women are encouraged not to focus on the home but instead, to have a career in the name of equality with men, it's got to be said communities are the worse for it. They are less warm, and less filled with life. However, we're now straying into a different kind of territory and a topic for another time.

I would finish this chapter by simply saying that the Woke gets it wrong when it tells women to ditch their femininity to be more like men. We don't need more men; we have enough of them already. And it doesn't make women more equal to mimic them. Women are equal as they are, from birth. And they flourish best not when trying to become more masculine, but when embracing their innate femininity—with all its empathy, patience, compassion, gentleness and relational warmth.

14
MARRIAGE BENEFITS ADULTS

We've spent the last couple of chapters talking about the unique strengths of men and women and that neatly leads us onto the next part of the Intersectional framework worth talking about—namely, marriage.

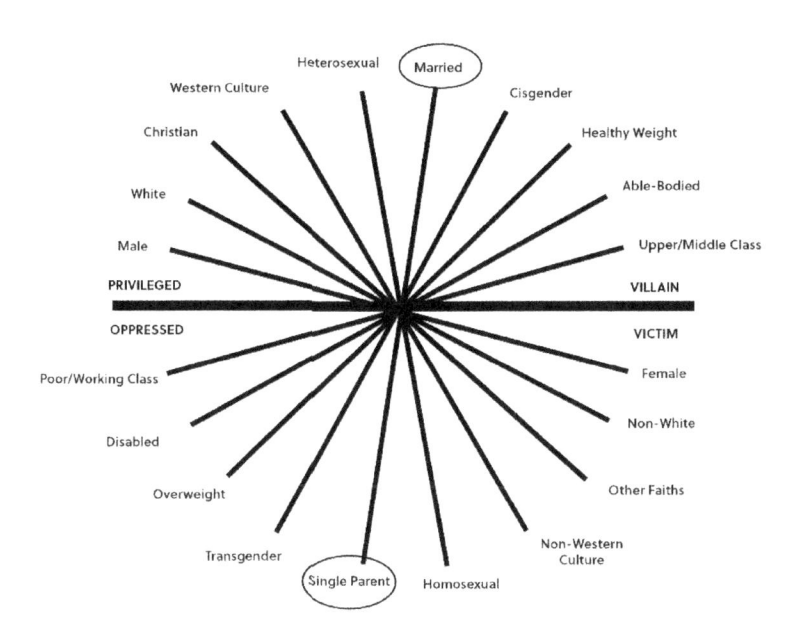

Diagram: Intersectional axis showing PRIVILEGED/VILLAIN vs OPPRESSED/VICTIM. Privileged/Villain side: Heterosexual, Married, Western Culture, Cisgender, Christian, Healthy Weight, White, Able-Bodied, Male, Upper/Middle Class. Oppressed/Victim side: Poor/Working Class, Female, Disabled, Non-White, Overweight, Other Faiths, Transgender, Non-Western Culture, Single Parent, Homosexual. "Married" and "Single Parent" are circled.

Traditionally, marriage has been considered the optimal setting for stability and happiness—for both men and women—as well as for the children they bring into the world. Conversely, single-parenthood has then traditionally been regarded as something sub-optimal at best; something shameful at worst. Sub-optimal because it means you're missing a spouse and that's not ideal for yourself or your children.

Shameful because it's suggestive of things like sex outside marriage, which was considered immoral even by the non-religious until the 1960s. Or perhaps because it suggests things like poor decision-making when choosing a spouse, or relational failure, or an inability to be a good husband or wife, or divorce. Because this was the traditional way of thinking, people traditionally strove to get married and stay married.

When the Woke came along and applied Intersectional Theory to the situation, they felt sorry for the single-parent. Identifying them as being marginalised in society, they sought to sympathise with them, champion their cause and offer them support. To that end, the Woke began proclaiming that single-parenthood should be considered in all ways equal to marriage. Single-parents shouldn't feel like they are in a sub-optimal situation and certainly they shouldn't feel ashamed. We should adjust our thinking and societal structures so that single-parenthood is considered equal.

Marriage Is Optimal

Here's the problem though. As difficult as it may be for single-parents to hear it, marriage *is*, in fact, optimal—both for men and women, and for children. And therefore, for wider society.

Firstly, let's look at how marriage benefits adult husbands and wives themselves. Marriage provides both partners with a sense of belonging, more opportunities for social engagement, and reduced feelings of loneliness.[1] As we saw in the previous chapter, this is especially true of men who struggle with loneliness without women to make connections. The increased loneliness of being single then has a knock-on effect on health outcomes. Lonely individuals are at significantly higher risk of developing serious health conditions such as stroke, diabetes, dementia, heart disease and arthritis. They are more likely to suffer from eating disorders, alcoholism and sleep deprivation. Overall, the health risks of loneliness are comparable to obesity and as dangerous as smoking 15 cigarettes a day.[2] A study of 2.2 million people around the world discovered that the risk of early death rises by 26% in the lonely. For these reasons, married men and women live on average, about two years longer than their unmarried counterparts and report better mental health along the way. Married people are on average less depressed, less anxious, and less psychologically distressed than their single counterparts. Indeed, married men are only half as likely as bachelors to commit suicide and are only one-third as likely compared to the divorced. 90% of married men who are alive at 48 will still be alive at 65. Only 60% of single men who are alive at 48 will still be alive at 65.

Marrying well not only makes us healthier; it makes us wealthier as well. Married men in the United States make between 4% and 32.6% more money compared to single guys—even controlling for education and job history.[3] And the longer a man stays married, the higher the marriage premium he receives. Some may suggest this is because women are simply more likely to marry high-earning men. However, studies have shown that doesn't fully explain it. There's something in a man that strives him to work harder and risk harder when he's aware his decisions are going to affect not only him, but his spouse as well. Having a wife gives a man a cause; a reason; a motivation; that pushes him on to maximise his potential. It should also be noted that women's earnings seemingly benefit from marriage...at least until children enter the picture. Childless wives will make up to 10% more than childless single women.

Married couples also tend to manage their finances better and build more wealth together than either would alone. At identical income levels for example, married people are less likely to report "economic hardship" or trouble paying basic bills. The longer you stay married, the more assets you will build. By interesting contrast, the length of *cohabitation* has no relationship to wealth accumulation—there is something specific to marriage alone that helps us build wealth. Around the year 2000, on the verge of retirement, the average American married couple had accumulated assets worth around $410,000 compared with $167,000 for the never-married and $154,000 for the divorced. Couples in one study who stayed married saw their assets increase twice as fast as those who had remained divorced over a five-year period.

Marriage lowers the risk that both men and women will become victims of violence. A Justice Department report discovered that single and divorced women are five times more likely to be victims of violence in any given year than wives. Single men were four times more likely to be violent-crime victims than husbands. Two-thirds of domestic violence crimes against women were committed by boyfriends, ex-boyfriends or ex-husbands, rather than husbands. One scholar summed up the relevant research on the topic saying, "Regardless of methodology, the studies yielded similar results: cohabitors engage in more violence than spouses."

Marriage increases relational stability by improving levels of fidelity. Cohabiting men are four times more likely to cheat on their partner than married men. Cohabiting women are eight times more likely to cheat than wives. Marriage then is in fact, the only realistic promise of permanence in a romantic relationship. Just 1 in 10 cohabiting couples are still together after five years. By contrast 80% of couples marrying for the first time are still together five years later. Despite the rising divorce rates of our times, around 60% of people will still marry for life, meaning that, although it's becoming riskier, it's still anyone's best bet for making love last.

An interesting theory put forward as to why men and women benefit from marriage so much is that it allows each gender to specialise—to each take on the life tasks that one person enjoys doing more than the other. Married households have twice the talent, twice the time, and twice the labour pool to begin with, and over time, and as they each assume specialised roles, they each begin to focus on their strengths. For example, as we saw earlier, men typically take on the burden of shovelling snow in the winter, doing repairs around the house, mowing the lawn and fixing the car. These are things he enjoys, but which a woman might find stressful. If the woman was single, she would have to deal with these things alone on top of everything else, but as a wife she doesn't. Remember the Expedite Robinson experiment where the guys revelled in being able to build a civilisation from scratch on a desert island while the women became stressed and began to cry? Now transport that general concept into the home. And of course, the reverse is true. While single men may find it stressful and complicated to form relationships, and to invest properly in them, a married man can delegate that task to his wife. Think of me getting stressed as I try to remember birthdays and having no idea what gifts to buy! This is a task I'd love to have a wife for. Single people have to do everything themselves—even the things they're not particular suited for. Married people can share the load and largely focus only on the things they love.

An article in the City Journal advocates for marriage saying, "Married people are both responsible for and responsible to another human being, and both halves of that dynamic lead the married to live more responsible, fruitful, and satisfying lives. Marriage is a transformative act, changing the way two people look at each other, at the future, and at their roles in society. And it changes the way significant others—from family to congregation to insurance companies—look at and treat the same couple. Sexual fidelity, an economic union, a parenting alliance, the promise of care that transcends day-to-day emotions: all these are what gives a few words mumbled before a clergyman or judge the power to change lives."

The same article goes on to encourage married couples to stick it out, even when times get hard. It says, "What proportion of unhappily married couples who stick it out stay miserable? The latest data shows that within five years, just 12% of very unhappily married couples who stick it out are still unhappy. 70% of the unhappiest couples now describe their marriage as "quite" or "very" happy. Just as good marriages go bad, bad marriages go good."

With all this data in mind, it's simply untrue to pretend that single-parents are not in a sub-optimal situation, and neither is it a good idea to say we should adjust our thinking and societal structures so that single-parenthood is considered equal. Very clearly, the best outcome for both sexes is to aim for marriage, and to do everything possible to stay married.

15
MARRIAGE BENEFITS KIDS

Now let's consider why marriage is also the best situation into which to bring children.

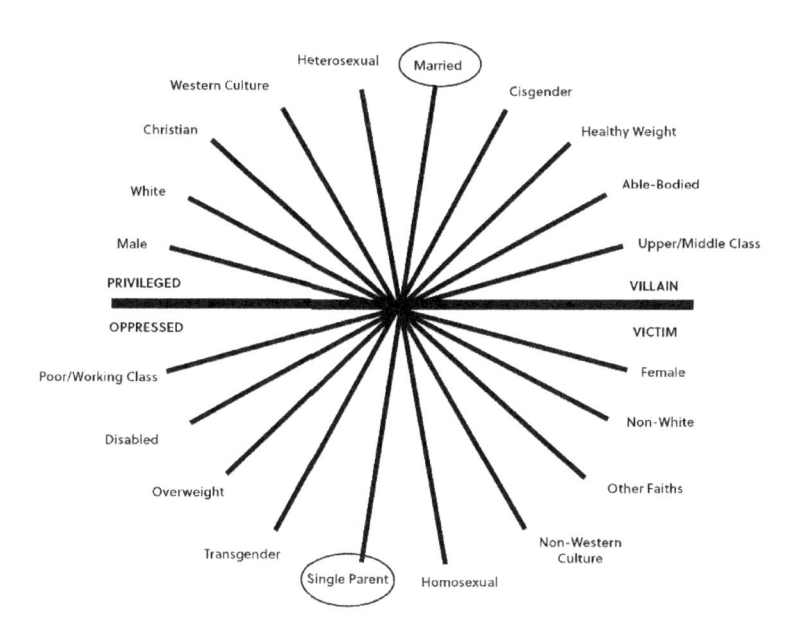

```
                        Heterosexual   Married
           Western Culture              Cisgender
        Christian                          Healthy Weight
      White                                  Able-Bodied
    Male                                       Upper/Middle Class
  PRIVILEGED                                      VILLAIN
  OPPRESSED                                       VICTIM
    Poor/Working Class                         Female
      Disabled                                Non-White
        Overweight                        Other Faiths
           Transgender              Non-Western
                    Single Parent  Homosexual   Culture
```

Given that 90% of single-parents are female, the majority of children in single-parent households are growing up without a present father.[1] Therefore, when I write this chapter I'm primarily thinking about the problems of single-motherhood. And that is a terrible thing for everyone involved. Especially the children. Indeed, if there's one incontestable body of evidence that exists about anything at all, it's that children need their dads.

The Importance of Fathers

According to the most recent US Census Bureau data, there are 18.4 million children in America living without a father—that's 1 in 4.[2] Research conducted by the same organisation, and others that I've provided in the bibliography, discovered that this affects those kids in the following ways:

Fatherless children have an infant mortality rate that is twice as high as fathered kids, and they are four times more likely to grow up in poverty. Indeed, around 47.6% of single-mother families—nearly half—are below the poverty line.[3] At preschool age, the verbal skills of fatherless kids will be significantly less-well developed. As they enter school, 85% of children with behavioural disorders come from fatherless homes. They are twice as likely to experience mental health problems like anxiety and depression. They are far more likely to experience psychosomatic physical health problems too—fatherless children report significantly more cases of chronic pain, asthma, headaches and stomach aches. They are 40% more likely to repeat a grade and 43% less likely to earn A's.[4] Fatherless children account for 71% of all high school dropouts, 90% of homeless and runaway children and 63% of youth suicides.[5] They are half as likely to go to college, 80% more likely to spend time in jail and since they are significantly more likely to engage in teenage sexual activity, they are 75% more likely to experience teenage pregnancy. Fatherless kids are twice as likely to have problems with obesity, while 75% of adolescents in substance abuse treatment facilities are from fatherless homes. 80% of adult rapists come from a fatherless home.[6] 70% of minors housed in state facilities are from fatherless homes. 90% of repeat offender arsonists come from fatherless homes. 85% of minors in prison come from fatherless homes. Up to 85% of gang members are from fatherless homes. They are also far more likely to suffer exploitation and abuse while growing up—fatherless children are five times more likely to experience physical abuse, and one hundred times more likely to experience fatal abuse. They are also 40% more likely to be sexually abused outside the safety of a fathered home.[7]

By the time the child becomes an adult then, their life outcomes will be significantly impoverished. They are significantly more likely to be unemployed, have low incomes, remain on social assistance, or experience homelessness. Their own romantic relationships will suffer as they are more likely to divorce or dissolve their cohabiting unions, and they are more likely to have children outside marriage themselves, thus perpetuating the problem of fatherlessness into the next generation. Finally, they are likely to have a lifespan which is on average, four years less than their fathered counterparts.

While I was researching these statistics, it brought to mind a CBS news report that went viral on social media in 2021. That year, at Southwood High School in Shreveport, Louisiana, there was a plague of violence that peaked when over the course of three days, 23 students were arrested for fighting.[8] Something of a crisis was emerging. However, as the CBS reporter noted some months later, it had suddenly all gone quiet: "Strangely, not a single incident has been reported since." Why? What was the reason for this miraculous turnaround? Dads. A group of fathers had come together to form "Dads on Duty." The reporter described them as "a group of about forty Southwood dads who now hang out at the school in shifts. Today, any negative energy that enters the building has to run a gauntlet of good parenting."

Several kids were asked on camera how the presence of the fathers at school had changed the atmosphere. One said, "I mainly feel a form of safety." Another said, "We stopped fighting, people started going to class." The reporter incredulously asked another, "how could that be?" She replied, "Have you ever heard of a 'look?'" The reporter asked, "A look? Dads have the power to do that?" Another student replied, "Yes! Not many people know it but they do. The school has just become a happy place to be and you can feel it." As well as the firm stares and stern warnings, the students noted how the dads had brought a sense of light-heartedness into the school with their "dad jokes" as well. It was that combination of authority and fun that almost instantly transformed the atmosphere of the school and brought it from a place of crisis to one of happy productivity.

Now take that concept and imagine it's applied to every home in the world. Instantly, almost miraculously, you would solve a huge proportion of the world's social problems. Not all of them. But a lot of them. The presence of dads is that important. Indeed, if we are to fix our broken society, it simply can't be done without placing the utmost importance on cohesive family units. That's the building block of a happy civilisation. Two parents, each looking after their kids, in their own way. Personally, I would say there's only one thing more important than that, and it's re-establishing widespread faith in Jesus Christ. Put God first, and family second, and the rest would largely fall into place.

Woke Destruction

One thing is for sure—given the weight of evidence for fathers is so overwhelming, it seems that ***deliberately*** bringing a child into the world as a single-parent, or doing anything that deliberately deprives a child of their father is incredibly negligent. Unfortunately, that's becoming more common. Women who have not been able to establish a solid marriage relationship with a man but who crave a baby, then deliberately choosing to bring one into the world themselves by way of artificial insemination. Likewise, men who deliberately walk out on their kids are equally to blame. The general culture of sex outside marriage which is so prevalent now—something the Bible unequivocally opposes—is also to blame. Kids need both their parents, anything less is sub-optimal, and given the kind of statistics we've been reading, that could be considered a euphemism.

Of course, it's not always the single-parent's fault. Sometimes husbands lose their lives and wives have no choice but to do it alone. Or vice versa. Sometimes men do abandon their responsibilities and never come back. Sometimes men are so abusive that the woman simply has to get out to protect her life and the life of her kids. To them, of course compassion, grace and support should be extended. They are doing heroic jobs trying to raise their kids without a teammate. But as we established in "Trench," in the attempt to extend grace, truth should never be sacrificed. And the truth is that children do best with fathers. That will always be the truth. There is something unique that each parent provides, and children suffer when deprived of either. In this chapter we've mainly been looking at fatherlessness, but motherlessness has its implications too. They're just not as widely felt in our society because it's a much rarer situation.

As hard as it will be to hear for many single-parents who are doing their best under difficult circumstances, for the well-being of the next generation, we mustn't start pretending that single-parenthood is anything less than sub-optimal. We must therefore re-establish in our society the Biblical principle that sex outside of marriage is immoral and dangerous. We must strongly promote the sanctity of marriage, and encourage people to get married always **before** bringing children into the world. We must encourage husbands and wives to stay married for the rest of their lives, as they promise to do in their vows, because this will provide the best life outcomes for themselves and for their children. They will be happier, healthier, wealthier and will live longer. All our governmental bodies, fiscal policies and tax structures should be configured to encourage and support marriage.

Because finally, this is best for wider society too. In 2010, the former British Conservative Party leader, Iain Duncan Smith, conducted a study to find out what the economic cost to the British economy was of fatherlessness. The total bill came out at £100 billion per year. Adjusting for inflation, we're now well above that figure. This he says, was calculated by looking at the cost to the taxpayer of all the extra social problems fatherless kids manifest—things like truancy, anti-social behaviour, teenage crime, addiction etc., as well as lost productivity and lower tax revenues that we know are a direct result of fatherless homes. When a father isn't there, effectively it's the tax payer that steps in to fund the child's upbringing.

When the Woke promote single-parenthood and encourage us to view it as equal to marriage, in many respects it may be with good intentions. They want single-parents to feel comforted, and for those who have fallen into this situation through no fault of their own, of course we should offer our full support. However, it's naïve and utterly destructive to deliberately pursue single-parenting as a lifestyle choice or to claim it has no effect on the children. Indeed, there are few things that destroy the fabric of the nation quicker than the destruction of the nuclear family unit. And of course, this is another reason why we must work against the hateful feminism that has driven a wedge between men and women, making them distrustful of one another. As we have already covered, the world needs both men and women operating in their respective masculinity and femininity. We work best as a team. We need each other and ideally, our kids need both their mums and their dads.

16
HOMOSEXUALITY

When I talk about the benefits of marriage, I am of course, talking about *heterosexual* marriage. Unfortunately, in this day and age, that needs to be clarified. And indeed, this is another part of life where Intersectionality has been destructive. Because of its influence, the Woke have tried to create "equality" between the sexual proclivities by pulling heterosexuality down and raising homosexuality up.

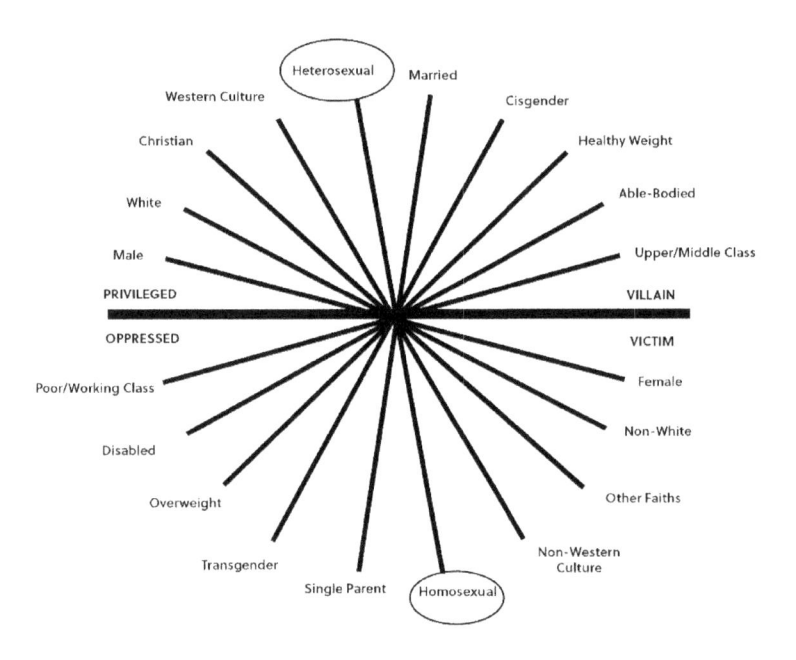

Diagram showing an intersectionality wheel with a horizontal axis labeled PRIVILEGED / VILLAIN on one side and OPPRESSED / VICTIM on the other. Spokes radiate from the center with labels: Heterosexual, Married, Cisgender, Healthy Weight, Able-Bodied, Upper/Middle Class, Female, Non-White, Other Faiths, Non-Western Culture, Homosexual, Single Parent, Transgender, Overweight, Disabled, Poor/Working Class, Male, White, Christian, Western Culture. "Heterosexual" and "Homosexual" are circled.

Earlier, we saw that the Woke would like to "smash heteronormativity" which is to say, they would like to abolish the idea that heterosexuality is the normal way of being. They believe it's the perceived normalcy of heterosexuality that makes homosexuality, by contrast, seem abnormal.

And yet, the simple truth is that heterosexuality *is* the normal way of being. According to the Office for National Statistics, in 2012, 94.4% of the British population identified as heterosexual.[1,2] This means that in a purely statistical sense, heterosexuality is **normal**. "Normal" is defined in the Cambridge dictionary as, "ordinary or usual; that which would be expected."[3] If you were to pick out a random person on the street, it would be overwhelmingly likely they are straight. Therefore, heterosexuality is normal. By extrapolating from that definition, homosexuality could then be considered **abnormal**—it is not the ordinary or usual. It is not what would be expected. Indeed, there is only a very small chance that a random person picked out on the street is going to be homosexual.

The reason for heterosexuality's prevalence is because it is furthermore, **natural**. "Natural" is defined in the dictionary as, "being in accordance with or determined by nature,"[4] and anyone with a basic understanding of biology understands that men and women are fundamentally designed for one another. As a plug is designed for a socket; as a lock is designed for a key; a man is designed for a woman. We've already spoken in this book about some of the ways in which the strengths and weaknesses of each sex are counter-balanced by the strengths and weaknesses of the other. And of course, it is only through sexual intercourse between men and women that life can be created and perpetuated on the earth. If all the earth turned to homosexuality tomorrow, there would be no life on it within 100 years. From pure logic then, we can say homosexuality is not self-sustaining and is in fact, destructive to life. Sexual orientation that doesn't conform to the natural configuration could then also be considered, "unnatural." That is what homosexuality is. By basic dictionary definition, it is abnormal and unnatural.

This is why the Woke want to promote it. According to the Intersectional framework, homosexuals as a minority group are to sympathised with, championed, and celebrated. To this end they loudly proclaim that homosexuality should be considered equal to heterosexuality in every way. By "smashing heteronormativity"[5] in order to tear it down, while celebrating homosexuality to raise it up, they are smashing the normal/natural while celebrating the abnormal/unnatural. This inversion wreaks destruction on society.

The Trauma Theory

Firstly, homosexuality wreaks destruction on the homosexuals themselves. Some years ago, I proposed "The Trauma Theory" on the Fuel Project YouTube channel. The theory says that homosexuality is caused by emotional trauma and psychological scarring in developmental years and it's really a sign of internal damage. To test the theory, I randomly chose ten gay celebrities and investigated their past to see if there was any evidence to support it. These celebrities were Ellen DeGeneres, Elton John, George Takei, Milo Yiannopoulos, Ricky Martin, Ruby Rose, Rosie O Donnell, Graham Norton, Tom Daly and Neil Patrick Harris. As I researched their past, I discovered that all but one of them but one had been sexually abused in childhood, or had been abandoned or abused by their fathers or step-fathers. The only person who bucked the trend was Neil Patrick Harris.

I'm not the only one to have noticed this link though. Indeed, many people who once considered themselves gay, but who now do not, have said it themselves. Milo Yiannopoulos has explicitly stated that he knows his homosexual feelings were a result of the sexual abuse he experienced as a child.

Jackie Hill-Perry is a prominent ex-lesbian who managed to find healing and she admits her homosexuality was in response to childhood abuse. She says, "Born with an inherent disposition to sin mixed with fatherlessness, molestation, and limited-to-no examples of trustworthy men led me into a lifestyle of homosexuality. It was a way of life I willingly embraced. My style of dress and behaviour was somewhat indicative of my personality. A girly-girl could never be used to describe Jackie. An aggressive tom-boy was more like it. Therefore, the girls I attracted were typically everything that allowed me to become what I thought I wanted to secretly be: a man. I always saw men as being something to envy. They seemed strong, powerful, in control. Femininity, or the skewed view of it that I held, seemed weak. Part of my embracing masculinity and rejecting femininity was my own way of protecting myself from pain—pain that I believed men were capable of subjecting me to. After all, that's what my father did to me. That's what I saw men do to my mother. That's what I witnessed my guy friends do to the women they claimed to love. All I knew of men was that they used their manliness as a means to inflict pain. And us women—us "weak beings"—were target practice."[6]

Another prominent example of an ex-gay who freely admits his feelings were rooted in trauma is Joseph Sciambra. He wrote, "Generally…gay men enter the lifestyle while in their late teens or early twenties. At that age, there are plenty of opportunities to express oneself and to experiment. This newfound power can be heady at first; for instance, you were once the kid that no one wanted on their team, or the boy with the overly critical and unloving father, or the scared child that someone touched. Suddenly, you are with people who have largely gone through the same thing, though almost never admitting it; instead, everyone plays out the trauma of youth in a bizarre ceremony of re-enactment as healing. Now, you can dance into the throng, feel their warm bodies next to you, and imagine that you are finally part of the group. Older men, who want you to call them daddy, ask you out; and that moment of shame and embarrassment from your childhood doesn't seem strange or horrifying anymore, because you can live it over again and draw pleasure from it under what you think are your own terms... Although I observed a genuine affection between [gay men], it was akin to the instant camaraderie which indelibly links all horror survivors. For, this was the characteristic that I witnessed in every same-sex couple: a bond of suffering enkindled by their shared memories of a childhood gone wrong: failed parents, tales of bullied boys and lonely nights spent crying out for love. It was a marriage forged through experience—of coming out, finding an introductory pride and hope in the gay lifestyle, then, seeing it dashed by the reality of collective gay self-centeredness and its propensity towards meaningless sex. They flee it, and by doing so, reveal its inherent dysfunction."[7]

I recently did an update to "The Trauma Theory" on YouTube and came across many comments from people across the world who continued to support the concept. One ex-gay man called Joel wrote, "Conversion therapy worked for me. My parents forced me and I was like, ok I can't change. I started talking about normal things in therapy and we did image therapy on trauma. My feelings eventually went towards women only."[8] Arletta wrote, "I have known both males and females who thought they were gay who got therapy for other things they considered emotional health issues and ended up realising they were not gay. They were just trying to find the kind of comfort they needed in a way that scared them less than other ways. All of them had been molested by at least one man when they were very young. Some, multiple men. Some, a man plus a woman or more than one woman, or multiple people of both sexes. I have never known anyone who is a homosexual who has not been molested and/or raped before they felt this was their state of being."

There are formal studies on this. According to a study by Vanderbilt University Medical Center and Vanderbilt University, 83% of lesbian, gay, bisexual and queer (LGBQ) individuals reported going through adverse childhood experiences such as sexual or emotional abuse.[9] The study involved 60,000 participants across eight states in the US. These findings supported an earlier study of 942 participants that found, "gay men and lesbian women reported a significantly higher rate of childhood molestation than did heterosexual men and women. 46% of the homosexual men in contrast to 7% of the heterosexual men reported homosexual molestation. 22% of the lesbian women in contrast to 1% of the heterosexual women reported homosexual molestation."[10] Another study from 2014 concluded, "Epidemiological studies find a positive association between physical and sexual abuse, neglect, and witnessing violence in childhood and same-sex sexuality in adulthood."[11]

The Destructiveness of Homosexuality

If we accept the huge weight of evidence that homosexuality is rooted in brokenness, of course it then becomes foolish to celebrate it like the Woke do. It's like celebrating someone for breaking their leg. Imagine going to a hospital with a broken leg and instead of healing it the doctor says, "aww we just want to accept you as the broken legged individual you are. We are pro broken legs in this hospital." What the homosexual really needs is not to be feted; they need to be healed. And urgently. Because the longer someone engages in homosexuality, the greater a toll this is likely to take on their emotional and physical well-being.

Indicative of inner brokenness, according to Mental Health America, those in the LGBTQ community are up to six-times more likely to experience symptoms of depression compared to heterosexual counterparts. They are more than twice as likely to feel suicidal, and more than four times as likely to attempt suicide.[12] Unsurprisingly then, they use mental health services at a rate that is 2.5 times higher than the heterosexual population and engage in higher rates of substance abuse. The Woke try to explain this by saying negative societal attitudes are the root of the mental health problems, but this doesn't stand up to scrutiny. In a time when homosexuality has never been so celebrated—there are literally parades on city streets, whole months dedicated to it, and rainbow flags worn and flown everywhere you look—mental health issues remain much more pronounced in the LGBTQ lifestyle. In truth, it is simply because they are living from a place of unrepaired brokenness that is in contravention of nature.

The physical risks of the homosexual lifestyle are no less pronounced. Centers for Disease Control and Prevention (CDC) says, "While anyone who has sex can get an STD, sexually active gay, bisexual and other men who have sex with men (MSM) are at greater risk."[13] For example, homosexual men are 86 times more likely to be diagnosed with HIV compared to straight men.[14] Even though homosexual men make up 2% of the American population, they make up 61% of the HIV infection. The CDC reports that 83% of syphilis cases in the United States are amongst gay man.[15] Similar results exist for Hepatitis B, chlamydia, gonorrhoea, genital warts and HPV (Human Papillomavirus) which is the most common STD in the US.

Gay men are 17 times more likely to get anal cancer compared to heterosexual men. Men who are HIV-positive are even more likely than that to get anal cancer. In general, gay men are twice as likely to get any kind of cancer compared to straight men, and on average, it happens a decade earlier.[16]

Such is the prevalence of disease that back in the 1990s, before medical science developed more effective treatments, it was estimated that engaging in the homosexual lifestyle would decrease a person's lifespan, on average, by between twenty and thirty years. In a 1998 study by the Family Research Institute in Colorado, they used four lines of research to investigate the average age of death of homosexuals compared to heterosexuals and concluded, "The four lines of evidence were consistent with previous findings suggesting homosexual activity may be associated with a lifespan shortened by 20 to 30 years."[17]

Due to improved treatments—especially for HIV/AIDS—homosexuals now tend to live longer than before. However, they still tend to die earlier than heterosexuals, and it must be remembered their slightly increased lifespan is only because we have learned to manage the inherent diseases through medicine—not because the lifestyle has become any less fraught with risk. Gay people are still overwhelmingly more likely to be living with disease than straight people.

Their relationships will be more unstable too—especially if they're men. Homosexual men are notoriously far more promiscuous than straight men and 79% of gay men report that over half of their sexual partners have been complete strangers. Fidelity amongst heterosexual married women is 85%, amongst heterosexual married men it's 75.5%, but amongst homosexual men it's only 4.5%.

Domestic violence rates are much higher too—nearly double, in fact. A 2014 study by Northwestern University involving 30,000 participants revealed that up to 75% of the homosexual population will experience domestic violence at some point in their lives.[18] The National Coalition Against Domestic Violence did their own studies and concluded for example, that women who have sex with women (WSW) are up to 26.1% more likely to suffer domestic abuse than heterosexual women. It all just speaks of brokenness.[19]

Once we understand this—that homosexuality is a consequence of trauma—and goes hand-in-hand with increased mental health problems, disease, shortened lifespans, instable relationships and increased domestic violence, to celebrate it like the Woke do ceases to be an act of compassion, but rather one of cruelty. As I said earlier, if someone presents with a broken leg, they don't need you to congratulate them for it or to insist that broken legs are just as valid as whole ones and they should be proud of it; what they really need, if possible, is healing. The same applies when someone presents with a broken sexuality. We've already established why it's a bad idea for the Woke to "smash heteronormativity" given that successful heterosexual marriage produces so many healthy outcomes for men, women and children. But hopefully what I've also established in this chapter is that it's a bad idea to raise up homosexuality too. Gay marriage shouldn't even be considered as an option.

Just as with all sins, there's an economic cost to homosexuality. Sexual health problems are estimated to cost the British tax payer around £700 million a year.[20] The cost of treating STDs is around £165 million a year and the lifetime treatment for every new HIV infection is anything up to £360,000. Given that homosexuality is the cause of the majority of these diseases—in some cases up to 83%—it is an outsized burden on the tax payer. When the Woke naively promote homosexuality, they are perpetuating emotional, physical and economic strain on everyone. The bottom line here is that you never create a healthy society by promotion any kind of brokenness. That's what they're doing here.

17
TRANSGENDERISM

In the same way the Woke would like to pull down heteronormativity to raise up and normalise homosexuality, the same applies to the issue of transgenderism. People who are "cisgender" are overwhelmingly the norm in society and therefore to create "equality" they are committed to pulling that down, while raising up the poor marginalised transgender community.

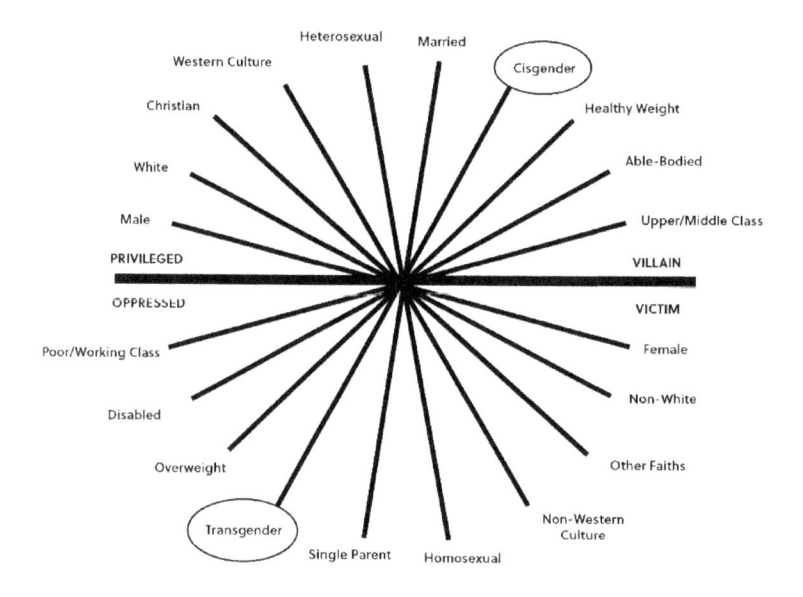

To be clear, using the definitions we established in the last chapter, transgenderism is unnatural and abnormal. In the 2021 UK Census, when asked, "Is the gender you identify with the same as your sex registered at birth?" only 0.5% of the population said, "no."[1] And to be just as clear, to believe that you are a different gender from the one you really are is to suffer from a disorder called *"**gender dysphoria.**"*

Medically, it can be said to be a kind of delusion. According to the John Hopkins Psychiatry Guide, the definition of "delusion" is "a fixed, false, idiosyncratic belief."[2] "Fixed" means the patient is certain about their belief and not persuaded by counter-arguments. "False" means the patient's beliefs aren't true. And "idiosyncratic" means the belief is characteristic of that individual patient. John Hopkins further explains that delusion is, "one of a trilogy of psychotic symptoms." The definition of "psychotic" or "psychosis" is "a severe mental illness characterised by defective or lost contact with reality."[3]

If then for example, a human woman has a fixed, false, idiosyncratic belief that she is a cat, she could be medically described as ***delusional*** and suffering from a form of ***psychosis***—she has lost contact with reality. If a man has a fixed, false, idiosyncratic belief he is Jesus Christ, then he is suffering from delusional psychosis. The same would apply if an adult man in his 50s started believing he was a 6-year-old girl; if a woman believed she was a dragon; or if a man believed he was a dog. These would all be examples of delusional psychosis. And indeed, these are all real life examples that have been in the news in recent years.[4]

Another example comes from an Edinburgh man called Nick O Halloran, who made headlines in 2017 when he presented an unusual form of delusional psychosis. Despite being healthy and having his limbs intact, he declared that he identified as an amputee.[5] Although he had two functioning legs, he said he felt that one of them didn't belong to him, and that he was a disabled person trapped inside an able person's body. Such was the hatred Nick had for his healthy leg, that he deliberately tried to injure it in horrific ways—for example, by injecting alcohol—so that doctors would have no choice but to cut it off. Of course, no surgeon in the UK would agree to amputate Nick's healthy leg because it was unethical to deliberately disable someone, and what they realised was that his leg wasn't really the problem…it was his mind. Nick's mind was broken. That's what needed to be addressed. He was suffering from delusional psychosis—he had a fixed, false, idiosyncratic belief that had caused him to disconnect from reality—and therefore, the best way to treat him was not through surgery but rather mental therapy.

Until 2013, gender dysphoria was officially considered a delusional psychosis in this fashion but due to the influence of Intersectional Theory, it was recategorized. The Woke said that the transgender community shouldn't be told they are disordered, but rather they should be celebrated and revered. Before 2013 then, if for example, a woman came forward claiming to believe she was a man born in the wrong body, and asked for hormone injections, breast amputation and genital surgery so that she could appear more like a man, the doctors would have treated her in much the same way as Nick O Halloran…or indeed a woman who thinks she's a cat or a dragon. They would have realised her mind was the problem and would have referred her to the psychiatric unit for mental therapy in the hope she could be healed and reconnected with reality. With the coming of Intersectionality Theory however, it was inevitable that attitudes would begin to change. Using this extremely flawed matrix, the Woke saw that transgender people were a marginalised minority and therefore, according to their belief system, were to be championed, revered, celebrated, and raised up. Correspondingly of course, as they were raised up, in the name of equality, "cisgender" people i.e. normal people without mental illness, had to be pulled down.

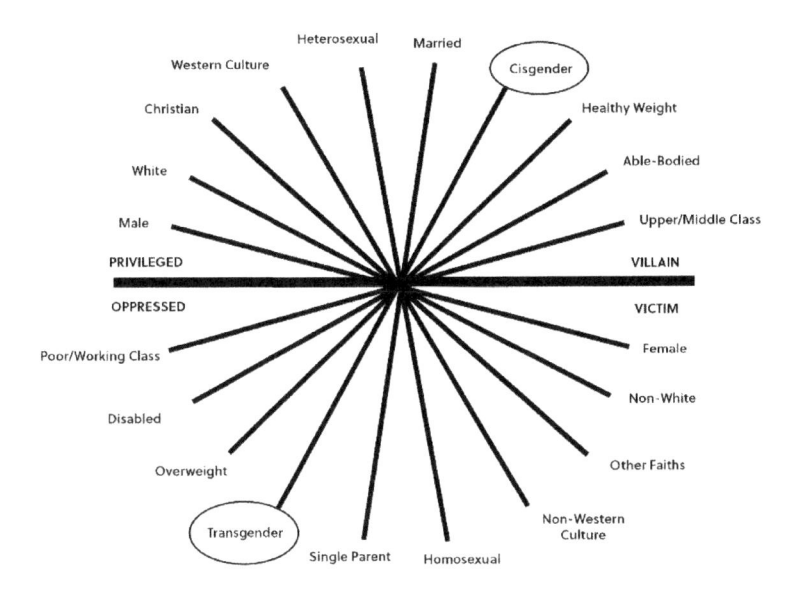

```
                    Heterosexual   Married
        Western Culture                    Cisgender
    Christian                                   Healthy Weight
                                                    Able-Bodied
       White
        Male                                        Upper/Middle Class
    PRIVILEGED                                      VILLAIN
    ═══════════════════════════════════════════════════════
    OPPRESSED                                       VICTIM
                                                    Female
    Poor/Working Class
                                                    Non-White
       Disabled
                                                   Other Faiths
            Overweight
                                            Non-Western
               Transgender                  Culture
                        Single Parent  Homosexual
```

Raising Up Transgenderism

"Raising up" transgenderism has happened in various ways. Firstly, instead of being referred to psychiatric units for mental treatment, people who claim to be trans are now very quickly fast-tracked towards hormone treatments and surgery in order to affirm their identity. There has also been a concerted attempt to try to normalise it in society as a whole, but especially amongst children. Books containing transgender propaganda have increasingly been targeted at kids, and have found their way into schools. In 2023 for example, it was discovered that a book called, "Call Me Max" which tells the story of a girl who wants to be a boy was being read aloud to children as young as four in the schools of America.[6] The idea has been pushed to children quite vociferously that humans can be born in the wrong body and it's a perfectly normal thing to want to switch. Indeed, the moment a child shows signs of not conforming to traditional gender roles e.g. a boy picks up a Barbie or a girl picks up a monster truck, they can now often be pushed by adults to believe they are transgender. Woke parents now often fizz with excitement at the idea their child might be trans because it's something of a status symbol in their community and it gives them a chance to virtue signal. Thus, children as young as nine have been prescribed sex-change hormones that block puberty and that set kids on a path towards surgery. This is especially prominent in Hollywood. Cher, Jennifer Lopez, Charlize Theron, Jamie Lee Curtis, Cynthia Nixon, Madonna and Megan Fox have all made it something of a trend to have a "trans kid."

In a further effort to normalise transgenderism amongst children, there has been a rise in the prominence of "drag queen story times" where men dressed as women tell stories and engage with young children…sometimes in very sexualised and provocative ways. Entertainment companies like Disney have started featuring trans characters in their movies. Celebrities have started cross-dressing to blur the lines. Men wearing dresses has been presented as "edgy" and "cool" in the media.

Raising up transgenderism has also meant allowing men who identify as women into women's spaces like bathrooms and locker rooms. It has meant admitting men into women's prisons. It has meant allowing men to compete against women in sporting events. And it has also meant, of course, many of the "prizes" that we looked at earlier in this book—status, position, platform, financial rewards, jobs and all the rest.

In 2022, the Scottish government even changed the law to accommodate transgenderism through the Gender Recognition Reform Bill. It meant that people could legally change their gender through "self-identification." Until then, a psychiatric diagnosis of gender dysphoria was required to be legally recognised as trans. No more. The bill meant that someone could on a whim, identify as the opposite sex and instantly have the full weight of the law behind them. In other words, one day a man could self-identify as a woman, and the next day he could stroll into a woman's locker room with the full support of the Scottish government. This has been done in other countries too.

Essentially then, society has been reconfigured around a mental illness. A delusion. A form of psychosis. And when you reconfigure society around mental illness, you produce chaos.

Chaos

In January 2023, a 31-year-old Scottish man called Adam Graham was convicted of raping two women. While the court case was ongoing, he took advantage of Scotland's new self-identification laws by declaring he was now a transgender woman called Isla Bryson. When the government heard about this, he was send to the female-only Prison Cornton Vale to fulfil his sentence.[7] That's right…they sent a male *rapist* into a female prison. Further investigations highlighted that he wasn't the first to game the system in this way—sixteen other men had done the same thing. At one point, the population of Cornton Vale also included Lennon (Katie) Dolatowski who had been convicted of sexually assaulting a 10-year-old girl. It also included Andrew (Tiffany)

Scott who is subject to a lifelong restriction order—something reserved for Scotland's most violent and dangerous offenders—after he admitted stalking a 13-year-old girl. All of these dudes had successfully managed to get into a woman's prison by manipulating the Gender Recognition Reform Bill.

There have been predictable consequences to putting male rapists in women's prisons. In 2018, a man called Stephen Wood was convicted of multiple rapes and sexual offences. He changed his name to Karen White to get admittance to a female prison. After being granted the switch, he promptly carried out a string of sexual assaults against the female inmates. Similar things have happened in the US as well. When Gender Self ID was introduced in the state of New Jersey for example, a man called Demetrius Minor changed his identity to Demi so he could get access to a female prison, whereupon he impregnated two other inmates.[9]

Allowing biological men to compete in women's sports has also introduced chaos. It has now become extremely common to hear of unremarkable male athletes switching to join women's teams and then using their innate physical advantage to dominate and break records. Women in swimming, track, basketball, cycling, football, rowing, golf, weightlifting, wrestling, volleyball and many other sports have had their own opportunities and rewards stolen in recent years because of such men. In the case of combat sports, it is of course extremely dangerous to let biological men and women face-off against one another. The most famous example thus far is of Fallon Fox—a biological man—who fought Tamikka Brents in a UFC cage fight. Fox beat Brents so badly that he broke her eye socket, causing it to require seven staples. Brents said that despite being an abnormally strong woman she had, "never felt so overpowered in her life."[10] In another example from the same sport, Alina McClaughlin (a man) choked his opponent into submission within two rounds.[11]

As for allowing males into female bathrooms, the chaos has been just as predictable there too. For example, in June 2023, the police were called to investigate a series of sexual assaults against girls that had taken place in "gender-neutral" toilets at a school in Essex, England. The culprit was a boy who was taking advantage of the free access.[12] In October, 2023 an American teenager and her parents filed a $30million lawsuit against the northern Virginia school system when a male student wearing a skirt walked into the female bathrooms and sexually assaulted her.[13]

The rush to push people towards hormones and surgery instead of psychiatric therapy has also backfired wildly. In 2020, a British woman called Keira Bell made headlines when she sued the British National Health Service (NHS) for transitioning her into a man. Having been something of a tomboy when she was a child, she approached the NHS at the age of sixteen for help, whereupon they immediately pronounced her as trans, and recommended a course of hormones and surgery. After experiencing deep regret for the transition, she said, "I should have been challenged on the proposals and claims I was making for myself. I think that would have made a big difference. If I was just challenged on the things I was saying. I was allowed to run with this idea that I had, almost like a fantasy, as a teenager…and it has affected me in the long run as an adult."[14] Indeed, with her body now permanently disfigured, her life has been hugely damaged.

Keira Bell's story is the tip of the ice-berg. In 2022, another British man who wished to remain anonymous underwent surgery, and upon waking up immediately realised he had made, "the biggest mistake of his life."[15] He said the doctors hadn't warned him of the drastic outcome of body-altering surgery, which had removed his genitals, left him infertile, incontinent, and feeling like a sexual eunuch. He has now stopped trying to be a woman and is suing the NHS for maltreatment.

There are many more stories like these. Lives ruined. Children being encouraged in their confusion by adults who should know better. Women being deprived of single sex spaces. Women being assaulted in bathrooms and prisons. Women being pushed out of their own sports; being deprived of their own opportunities and rewards; being severely injured by having to compete against men.

Something that we've not discussed yet is also how perfectly competent and good people are now being fired from their jobs for failing to play along with the delusions. There's the story pf David Mackerith for example—a doctor of 26 years who was fired because he refused to call a 6 foot bearded man, "madam." Good Christian teachers like Joshua Sutcliffe were also banned from the classroom for "misgendering" pupils who had, on a whim, decided to cause chaos by pretending they were the opposite sex from what they were.[16]

This is what happens when, instead of treating gender dysphoria as the mental illness that it is, you instead reconfigure society around it. When you allow people suffering from delusional psychosis to call the shots, dictate company policy, shape public discourse, reconfigure public services and utilities, as well school curriculums and government policy, it is, in a very real sense, allowing the lunatics to run the asylum. The mentally ill do not make good decisions. It will only produce chaos.

18
CONTAGION

Let's stay on the issue of transgenderism for another chapter and discuss how trying to normalise it is spreading sexual confusion around our society, especially amongst the younger generations. You see, all those efforts to target the kids with propaganda as discussed in the last chapter is having something of an effect.

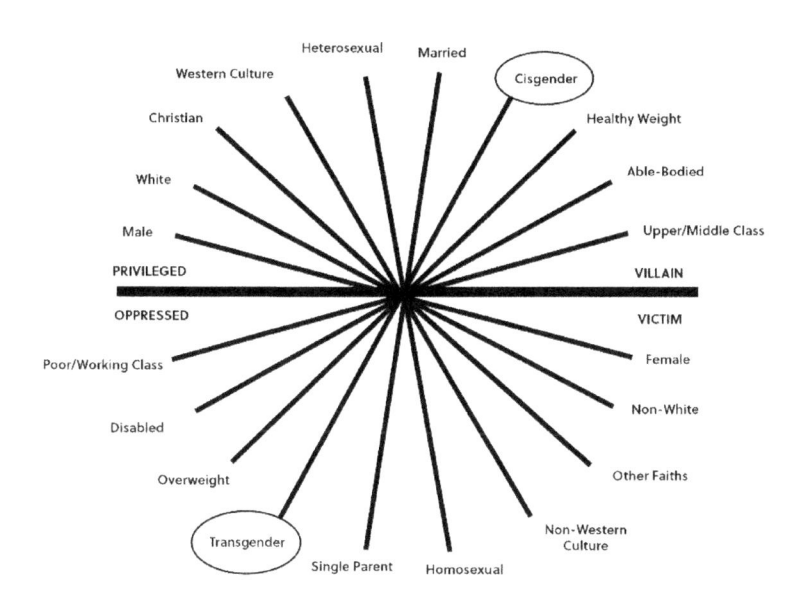

Diagram: A star/radial chart with axes labelled PRIVILEGED/VILLAIN (top) and OPPRESSED/VICTIM (bottom). Spokes are labelled: Heterosexual, Married, Cisgender, Healthy Weight, Able-Bodied, Upper/Middle Class, Western Culture, Christian, White, Male, Female, Non-White, Other Faiths, Non-Western Culture, Homosexual, Single Parent, Transgender, Overweight, Disabled, Poor/Working Class. "Cisgender" and "Transgender" are circled.

In recent years, the news has been filled with stories about a shocking rise in young people who have abandoned heterosexuality to claim a place in the LGBTQ community. In 2021 for example, Ipsos released the results of a worldwide survey that said nearly 18% of Gen Z'ers (those born after 1997) now identify as something other than heterosexual. A further 14% said they didn't know or preferred not to say. Therefore, only 68% of that age group were willing to explicitly identify as heterosexual.[1] This is in stark contrast to previous generations who were almost exclusively heterosexual and where LGBTQ identification was a tiny minority. Another survey conducted a year later by Gallup nudged the figures upwards saying that 20.8% of Gen Z now identified as belonging to the LGBTQ community in some way. Again, this is a sharp rise on previous generations where 10.5% of Millennials (1981-1996), 4.2% of Gen X (1965-1980), 2.6% of Baby Boomers (1946-1964), and 0.8% of Traditionalists (before 1946) identified as LGBTQ.

Perhaps the biggest rise in sexual confusion has come in regard to transgenderism. According to a 2012 study commissioned by NHS England, that year there were just under 250 referrals, most of them boys, to the Gender Identity Development Service (GIDS), run by the Tavistock and Portman NHS foundation trust in London. By 2022 however—ten years later—there were more than 5,000 referrals. This is nearly a 2000% increase. And this in itself, was twice as much as the previous year.[2] So sudden has this increase been, especially amongst young girls, that a team of NHS researchers were tasked with investigating the problem. One London-based psychiatrist said, "In the past few years it has become an explosion. Many of us feel confused by what has happened, and it's often hard to talk to colleagues."[2] The unnamed consultant, who had been practicing in a child and adolescent mental health unit for seventeen years continued, "I might have seen one child with gender dysphoria once every two years when I started practising. It was very niche and rare. Now somewhere between 10% to 20% of my caseload is made up of adolescents registered as female at birth who identify as non-binary or trans." Another senior child psychiatrist said, "In the last five to 10 years we've seen a huge surge in young women who, at the age of around 12 or 13, want to become boys. They've changed their name and they are pressing…to have hormones or puberty blockers. Often those girls are children who are going through the normal identity and developmental problems of adolescence and finding a solution for themselves in this way."

Miriam Grossman MD is a child and adolescent psychiatrist who has explored the issue in depth and authored five books on the subject. In 2023, she released a book called "Lost In Trans Nation—A Child Psychiatrist's Guide Out of the Madness," where she examined why there was such a rise in young people—again, especially girls—trying to claim a transgender identity. Speaking about the subject on the Triggernometry podcast, she said, "We have a new group; a new demographic; mostly girls; still a lot of boys [and we coined the term for them] 'Rapid Onset Gender Dysphoria.' This is a group, mostly young girls, who never before expressed any discomfort with being a girl. Who over a short period of time, and following immersion in the internet and social media…and most of them also have at least one or multiple pre-existing psychiatric problems…by that I mean, they are on the autism spectrum; they have anxiety disorders; they have social phobia; depression; they may have self-injury, they may be cutting themselves; they may have gone through some trauma in their life….they are led to believe that if they don't feel comfortable with themselves…they may be a boy. And of course, you get a lot of points for this. Your status is elevated when you come out as non-male-or-female…If you come out to your friends as being neither male or female, you're placed in an elevated status."[3]

Grossman here confirms that according to what she's seen as a child psychiatrist, at least part of the explanation for the explosion of transgenderism, is that many young people are now competing in the Victimhood Olympics. Young people have understood that if they claim a minority identity, their status is going to be elevated in school, both amongst teachers, with their peers, and indeed with the wider world. They will suddenly become the most revered person in any room. They will often be given carte blanche with their behaviour, they will likely evade punishment for misbehaviour, and they will be given perks and platform. They will be indulged and celebrated in ways that ordinary students won't.

Grossman continues, "Not only that, but you see, if you are a white, heterosexual, middle-class or upper-class student, you're an 'oppressor.' Now, you don't want to be an oppressor. You want to be oppressed. So if you are a member of a sexual minority or another minority…you can't change your race; you can't change your socio-economic status; you're not going to come out and say you're gay or lesbian if you're not…but to say you're neither male or female [is an easy path.]³

Here, Grossman confirms the direct role that pervasive Intersectional Theory is playing in the mindsets of young people today. Having had their heads filled with this ideology, children have realised that if they are white, heterosexual, middle-class, and normal in every other way, they are by the theory's reckoning an irredeemably evil villain.

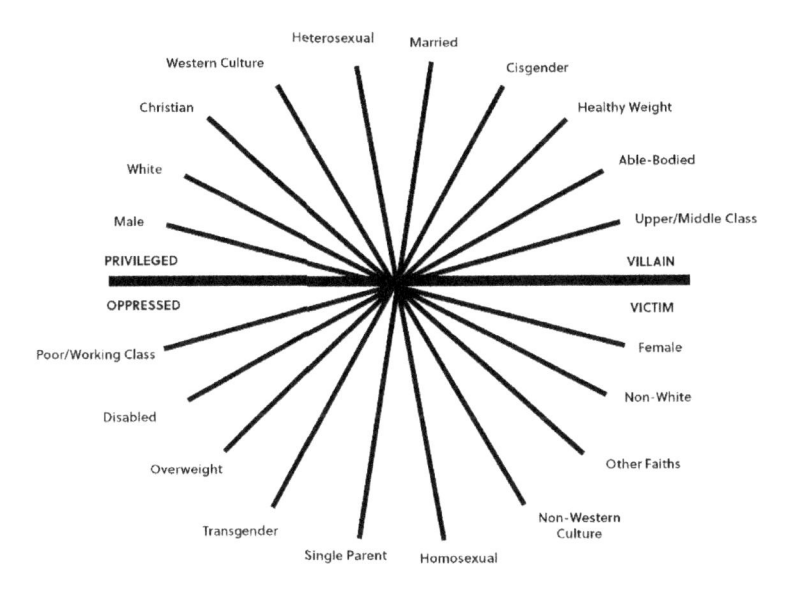

```
                    Heterosexual   Married
       Western Culture    \    |    /   Cisgender
         Christian         \   |   /    Healthy Weight
            White           \  |  /     Able-Bodied
             Male            \ | /      Upper/Middle Class
       PRIVILEGED ═══════════════════════════ VILLAIN
       OPPRESSED                              VICTIM
    Poor/Working Class    / | \              Female
           Disabled      /  |  \            Non-White
         Overweight     /   |   \          Other Faiths
       Transgender     /    |    \       Non-Western Culture
                 Single Parent   Homosexual
```

Of course, they don't want to be an evil villain. They don't want to be the problem. They don't want to be worthy of all hatred, or to feel that their mere existence is preventing an egalitarian and peaceful utopia from emerging on the earth. They want to be on the other side of the horizontal line. Therefore, according to Grossman, they are deliberately and desperately trying to find something to change about their identity that will provide redemption—something that will move them from 'oppressor' to 'oppressed.' Something that will move them from "villain" to "victim." How can they claim victimhood for something? The easiest way to do this, Grossman suggests, is simply to identify as non-binary and claim an unusual gender identity.

    This partially explains why transgenderism has become a kind of contagion in the Gen Z demographic. And although Grossman says young people aren't going to come out and say they're gay or lesbian if they're not, I disagree. I think a significant reason why we're seeing a spike of Gen Z'ers now claiming LGBTQ status is also because of this motive. It's a generation of kids who have perniciously been convinced by Intersectionality that they're inherently evil, and who are therefore desperate to find something about themselves that will give them some kind of redemption. They're scrambling to get under the horizontal line somehow, and weird sexuality is the easiest way to do it.

The Mental Disorder Connection

Something that Grossman alludes to is that kids with pre-existing mental health problems—anxiety, social phobia, depression etc.—are especially susceptible to this contagion. Nearly all of the referrals she has seen for gender dysphoria have come with one of these pre-existing conditions. Although it's a slight diversion from the train of thought we are on, we should ask ourselves why so many Gen Z children today are experiencing such an increase in mental health issues that leaves them susceptible to these sexual identity problems.

To that end, I would argue that it can largely be explained by the breakdown of the nuclear family unit. Earlier we saw the importance of fathers in children's lives and how because of their absence, so many children are now struggling in a myriad of ways. According to a study by the University of Bristol and funded by the UK Medical Research Council, girls with absent fathers during early childhood are 53% more likely to suffer from anxiety and depression in adolescence.[5] This, I believe, is clearly feeding into their susceptibility to sexual identity confusion. A report by the Centre for Social Justice declared, "The increase in cases of mental illness in Britain can in part be attributed to the high levels of family breakdown…Family breakdown has the biggest adverse impact on children's well-being...Children with separated, single, or step-parents are 50% more likely to fail at school, have low self-esteem, experience poor peer relationships and have behavioural difficulties, anxiety or depression."[5] Broken families, and fatherlessness is also a predictor of homosexual behaviour later in life.

In short, family breakdown is creating children who are increasingly suffering from mental health problems, and these mental health problems in turn leave them especially vulnerable to identity confusion. They are then encountering the world of Intersectional Theory which promises they can be healed of their brokenness, and redeemed them of their inherent evil, and given status in the world if they embrace LGBTQ ideology. Although it's only part of the story, is it any wonder then, that there has been such an explosion of homosexuality and transgenderism in the world today? It is pushing kids towards embracing a delusional psychosis, and this isn't a pathway to a healthy future society.

19
CHRISTIANITY

Because Christianity has been the most commonly held faith in the West for many centuries, Intersectional Theory considers it privileged, and in the name of equality, something therefore to be pulled down. By the same token, every other minority faith system is to be celebrated and raised up.

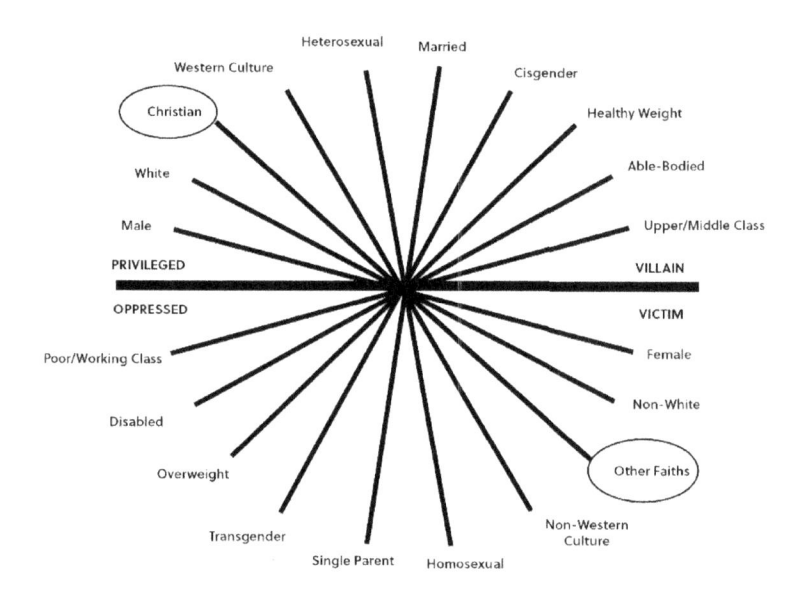

The Growing Hatred of Christianity

There are many reasons why it's natural for the Woke to hate Christianity. Christians tend to stand up for heterosexuality while speaking against homosexuality; we tend to be pro-marriage and traditional family units; and hold to a Biblical definition of male and female. These are all beliefs that stand in opposition to Intersectional Theory. Christians also tend to be certain that what we believe is true, and therefore by the same token, we believe other faiths are false. To the Woke, that won't do. That perpetuates inequality. Christians then, by their very existence, are seen as a barrier to the egalitarian utopia the Woke think they're building.

The hatred of Christianity in the West has passed through several phases since Intersectionality first began to take hold in the early 1990s. It began as mere ***caricaturization*** designed to make Christians look like clownish buffoons—think of people like Ned Flanders in The Simpsons as an example. Essentially they were portrayed as harmless but not to be taken seriously.

That which has been caricaturized can then however easily be ***marginalised***. Increasingly people began to say that Christianity is fine for people as long as it's conducted behind closed doors, but that it should have no place in public life. For example, in a 2015 essay for Slate, Brian Palmer wrote about how, when an outbreak of Ebola gripped the African continent, Christian missionary doctors flooded in to help. Palmer expressed "ambivalence," "suspicion," and "visceral discomfort" about the fact these Christian men and women were motivated to make "long-term commitments to address the health problems of these Africans," to "risk their lives," and accept poor compensation (and sometimes none at all) because of their faith.[1] Why was Palmer worried about this? Surely this was nothing but a beautiful thing? Well, Palmer admitted he was concerned that since they were motivated by God to help heal the sick, they might actually talk about him to the patients at the time same, and thus perpetuate Christian beliefs. He said, "It's great that these people are doing God's work, but do they have to talk about him so much?" This is indicative of the views people began to hold more widely in the West. "You can have your Jesus behind closed doors, but don't dare talk about him in public or bring him into the open."

The marginalisation then gradually spilled into *vilification*, *villainization*, and then *criminalisation*. Barely a month goes by without a story hitting the headlines in this respect. In 2011, a Christian café owner in Blackpool, England was threatened with arrest by the police for displaying Bible verses on a screen.[2] In 2014, a gay rights activist called Gareth Lee started a campaign to sue the Christian Ashers bakery in Northern Ireland because they refused to bake a cake supporting gay marriage.[3] In 2016, a UK Christian couple were blocked from adopting or fostering children because of their views on homosexuality.[4] In 2019, David Mackerith was fired after 26 years in his job as a doctor because he said in good-conscience, as a Bible-believing Christian, he couldn't submit to transgender ideology and call a 6ft bearded man, "madam."[5] In 2018 a Christian nurse was sacked in Britain for giving one of her cancer patients a Bible.[6] In 2022, another Christian nurse was fired for wearing a cross necklace. In 2023, a Christian teacher was fired for "misgendering" a trans pupil.[7] There are regular stories of the police arresting Christian street-preachers.[8] Therein we see belief in Jesus, and preaching of the Bible, is no longer just caricatured or even marginalised; it's now vilified and considered criminal behaviour to speak freely about your faith. Indeed, the message is coming through loud and clear from the Woke establishment…there is no place for you in this society.

The hatred can be visceral. "If Jesus comes back, kill him again"[9] became a meme which started appearing online and on t-shirts around 2016. Don Crawford encountered a Woke American citizen in

2022 who apparently told him, "I hate Christianity as much as I hate America."[10] We'll talk more about why a Woke American would hate his own country shortly, but the contempt which they show towards Christianity is worth examining because this is the single biggest reason for our civilisation's demise. The day the West began to tear down Christianity was the day it began sowing the seeds of its own destruction. I don't have the space to go into detail here—though I have done so in other books and series, so if the subject interests you I encourage you to explore those. But in the meantime, let me give a brief overview of why Christianity should retain its privileged position in Western society.

How Christianity Made The West

I'm not overstating it when I say there has been no more powerful force for good in the world—especially the West—than Christianity, and the evidence for that is almost never-ending.

Christianity was the power that ended infanticide in the West—the killing of babies—something that was extremely prevalent in the Greco-Roman world. The Carthaginians sacrificed babies. Plutarch says they "offered up their own children, and those who had no children would buy little ones from poor people and cut their throats."[11] The Romans believed disabled babies should be destroyed. Cicero said, "deformed infants shall be killed." Even Seneca, who was considered to be more morally advanced for his time said, "We drown children who at birth are weakly and abnormal." So rampant was infanticide that Polybius blamed the decline of the population in ancient Greece on it. The practice only waned because of Christians who taught from the Bible that all murder is wrong, and that all human life is valuable to God and made in His image.

Christianity similarly ended the routine practice of infant abandonment, which was equally common in the Greco-Roman world, and was even written deeply into their legends. The founders of Rome—Romulus and Remus—were said to be boys who had survived being tossed into the Tiber River. One of the most famous ancient Greek plays, Oedipus Rex revolves around a boy who was abandoned at three days old. Christians were the first to oppose this practice and they were even the first to establish orphanages and drop-off locations for unwanted babies, who would then be raised by the church.

In the Greco-Roman world, humans were often killed for entertainment in the form of gladiatorial shows. For hundreds of years, the citizens of Rome had watched countless gladiators mauled, mangled and gored to death while thinking nothing of it, viewing their lives as expendable and cheap. Indeed, each gladiator was viewed as, "crude, loathsome, doomed, lost…a man utterly debased by fortune, a slave, a man altogether without worth or dignity, almost without humanity."[11] Who was responsible for the ending of this barbaric practice? Christians. At first their opposition infuriated the Romans. Minucius Felix wrote, "You do not go to our shows; you take no part in our processions…you shrink in horror from our sacred [gladiatorial] games." However, ultimately, the Christian influence prevailed and the games were banned.

Human sacrifice was a widespread in many parts of the world before Christianity. The Druids of Ireland and Scotland did it. The Prussians and Lithuanians did it. The Aztecs and Mayans of South America did it. In their circumstance, they would even eat the flesh of the sacrificed. Bernal Diaz del Castillo, a Conquistador who survived capture at the hands of the Mayans said his compatriots were eaten, "with a sauce of peppers and tomatoes. They sacrificed all our men in this way, eating their legs and arms, offering their hearts and blood to their idols." When did these barbaric practices end? With the arrival of Christianity.

Paedophilia was common in the ancient world, especially amongst the Greeks and Romans. It is seen in the literature of their poets and philosophers, as well as depicted on archaeological artifacts that survive to this day. Bestiality was also reasonably common. Apuleius, a second century Latin author, describes wealthy Romans having sex with donkeys and a woman called Pasiphae consorting with a bull. Christianity was responsible for bringing a new sense of sexual purity.

Christians introduced the modern idea of charity. **Liberalitas** was the common way of things in Pre-Christian Rome. It meant giving with the expectation that the recipient would return the favour. Jesus however had said, "If you lend to those from whom you expect repayment, what credit is that to you? Even sinners lend to sinners, expecting to be repaid in full. But love your enemies, do good to them, and lend to them without expecting to get anything back." (Luke 6:34-35) With this teaching ringing in their ears, Christians switched away from liberalitas to *caritas*—giving without expecting anything in return, merely to show love and compassion. And hence almost all the oldest charitable organisations in the West trace their origins to Christian founders.

In the first three centuries after Christ, Christians began building the modern concept of hospitals to care for the sick. Medical nursing is therefore a Christian innovation. It's notable that when a series of plagues hit Rome in the 1st and 2nd centuries, the pagan

Romans, as was their custom, fled to escape, abandoning the sick to their fate. The only ones that stayed behind to care for the sick were Christians who no longer feared death. As a result of these actions, Christianity boomed in popularity.

Christians were the first to educate both sexes—not only men—and to give dignity to women in this way. Christians were the first to create the idea of tax-funded schools. They were the first to create the idea of education for the deaf. Indeed, Michel de L'Epee, the man who developed sign language, was an ordained minister. The same goes for the blind. Louis Braille was a dedicated Christian who invented a way for the blind to read through their fingertips. Christians invented Sunday Schools primarily as a way to give the poor free education. Christians were at the root of the child labour laws of the 1800s that made sure children were no longer exploited. Christians were the originators of most university establishments we know today, especially in the United States. They were at the root of the ideas about property rights and individual freedoms. It was Christians who signed the Magna Carta which is generally recognised to be the foundational document of modern Western ideas of liberty and justice. As I touched upon earlier, it was Christians, especially the Clapham Sect led by William Wilberforce, who abolished slavery in the British Empire and who then used the might of the Empire to stop it around the world. It's Christians who gave us some of the most impressive architecture in Western civilisation. It's also Christians who gave us some of the finest artworks and music.

So successful was Christianity at reforming societies, that by the 20th Century, the nations where it had been most widely practiced were also the least corrupt, the healthiest, the happiest and the most prosperous nations on earth. This has been proven by multiple studies.

More recent surveys have proven Christians are twice as likely to engage in charitable giving than atheists.[12] Christians are also more likely to volunteer their time to good causes. Christianity has proven uniquely capable amongst all the religions of the world in creating the kind of societies people enjoy and actually want to live in.

In many ways then, Christianity is a victim of its own success. Its ideas have been so successful, and saturated so much of Western thinking, that people born into this culture no longer connect the ideas with their origin at all—that origin being Jesus. It's a bit like Shakespeare. William Shakespeare invented phrases that forever changed the English language. "Puking," "vanish into thin air," "There's a method to my madness," "Wild goose chase," "Break the ice," "The green-eyed monster," "Wear my heart upon my sleeve," and many others came from Shakespeare.[13] We all use these phrases but we almost never realise they originated with him because they're now so commonplace. Likewise, we all now believe infanticide and child abandonment is wrong, that killing for entertainment is wrong, that paedophilia is wrong, that slavery is wrong, that the sick and the orphan should be cared for, yet we do these things never realising that these ideas all came from Jesus.

Tom Holland is an historian who explored the Greco-Roman world and was curious to find so many assumptions and practices in that time that were completely alien to him. What had happened for him to feel so differently from the people of 2000 years ago? In his explorations he came upon an undeniable truth. It was Christianity. Christianity had changed the world. He said, "People in the West, even those who may imagine that they have emancipated themselves from Christian belief, in fact, are shot through with Christian assumptions about almost everything…All of us in the West are goldfish, and the water we swim in is Christianity."[14]

To tear down Christianity then, as the Woke are attempting to do, is to tear down the very thing that made our civilisation and that gave us all our best ideas, values and assumptions. It's to destroy the very thing that made us good and that caused our society to thrive. It's a bit like setting fire to the house in which you live. The problem with trying to equalise the faiths is that they're not all equal. Ideas never are. There are good ideas and there are bad ones. Christianity traditionally gained a unique position of honour in the West amongst our ancestors primarily because it's true but secondly because they could see that it was full of good ideas. They saw that when its precepts were applied, it created a beautiful place to live. In short, Christianity worked. The other faiths? Not so much.

20
OTHER FAITHS aka ISLAM

There are some religious ideas that simply shouldn't be raised up and this is another problem of Wokeism. Intersectional Theory doesn't examine the merits of the religions and then make individual judgements about the strength of the ideas they contain; rather it takes a very simplistic view that whatever is in a minority should be celebrated regardless of what the religion actually promotes. In raising up any faith that isn't Christianity, for the sole reason it isn't Christianity, it raises up bad ones. I'm going to focus on Islam in this chapter because as I write, it's the most significant minority in the Western world. It also represents the biggest threat.

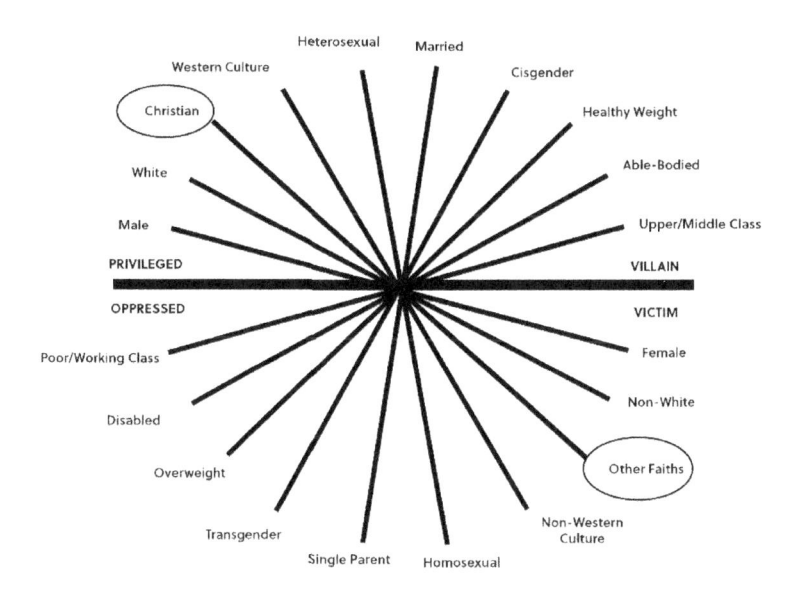

At the time of writing in late 2023, there is something of a political crisis emerging whereby hundreds of predominantly young men from Islamic regions of the Middle East and North Africa are making their way illegally into Europe. The United Kingdom seems to be an especially enticing destination, and therefore hundreds, if not thousands, of them are daily crossing the English Channel to arrive on beaches in small boats. According to official British government statistics, in the year 2022, net migration to the UK was 745,000 and a large number had entered illegally by this small boat method.[1,2]

The Woke, of course, welcome them with open arms. To them, these are a poor, marginalised, minority who perfectly meet their criteria for support and compassion. However, the truth is that the ideology they carry in their heads and hearts is simply incompatible with the British values we inherited from Christianity, and which made the West. Furthermore, they have no intention of assimilating to our ways, but rather hope to impose Islam upon us.

I made a video about this recently on The Fuel Project, so apologise if this is repeated information. But I think the best way of exposing the dangerous nature of the Islamic ideology is to look at the life of its founding prophet, Muhammad. Once we understand who he was, we understand the actions of those who follow him.

The Life of Muhammad

Muhammad was born in 570AD in Mecca, which is in modern day Saudi Arabia. Mecca at that time was a polytheistic society and there were around 360 different gods being worshipped by the local pagan tribes there. Idols were crafted for each one and they were placed inside a big cube called the "Kabbah" which became the centre of the city's worship.

Amongst the pagan gods that were worshipped at the Kabbah was one called "Allah." Allah was not considered the sole divinity by the Meccans; he was just one of hundreds of gods. Interestingly, he was believed to have kinship with the jinn, which is the Islamic word for demons.[2] Allah was worshipped by Muhammad's family and indeed, his father was called Abd-Allah (or Abdullah) which means, "the slave of Allah."[3] Unfortunately for Muhammad, he never knew his father because he died from illness before he was born. To add to the sorrow, his mother then died when he was only six-years-old. As an orphan, he was then sent to be raised firstly by his grandfather for two years, then after he died, his uncle—a merchant called Abu Talib.

Abu Talib was not a particularly successful merchant and most biographies will mention his poverty.[4] Muhammad however, spent the next 17 years or so following Abu Talib as he traded around the region, learning how to buy and sell. During those early years Muhammad received no education. He never learned to read or write. Muhammad was illiterate.

At 25, through these trading journeys with his uncle, he met a very wealthy tradeswoman called Khadija. Khadija was born into a wealthy dynasty but she had taken over the family business and had been very successful at it. Before long, Muhammad and Khadija were married. Khadija was considerably older than Muhammad—most traditions say she was 40, but financially, this was a great deal for him. After growing up in relative poverty as an orphan with his uncle, he was now able to live in the lap of luxury.

By the time Muhammad reached the age of 40 himself however, it seems he went through something of a midlife crisis. He had lots of wealth through his marriage to Khadija but it seemed he began looking for more significance and he began focusing on more transcendent issues. It's around this time, he started wandering off by himself into the desert for extended periods, where he would find caves to meditate and pray in. His favourite cave was at a place called Hira, which is to the north of Mecca, around two hours walk away. He would spend days at a time hidden there—only coming back home when he was hungry, to stock up on food. And it was during one of these trips to Hira that he had a distressing supernatural experience with an angel.

The hadith—the Islamic texts that record the words and deeds of Muhammad—report what happened. Sahih Bukhari, which is considered one of the two most authoritative hadiths along with Sahih Muslim says, "[Muhammad] used to go in seclusion to the cave of Hira where he worshipped continuously for many days and nights. He used to take with him the journey food for that stay and then come back to his wife Khadija to take his food like-wise again for another period to stay, till suddenly the Truth descended upon him while he was in the cave of Hira. An angel came to him in it and asked him to read. The Prophet replied, "I do not know how to read." The Prophet added, "The angel caught me forcefully and pressed me so hard that I could not bear it anymore. He then released me and again asked me to read, and I replied, "I do not know how to read." (Bukhari 6982) The angel then attacked Muhammad two more times before in abject panic, he escaped and fled back home. It says he burst through the door, "his neck muscles twitching with terror till he entered upon Khadija and said, "cover me! Cover me!" They covered him till his fear was over and then he said, "O Khadija, what is wrong with me?" (Bukhari 6982)

Muhammad was so shaken by this incident in the cave that he was afraid of what was happening to him. He thought he was either going insane or he was being possessed by demonic spirits. Khadija tried to calm him down but when Muhammad remained filled with terror, she took him to see her cousin, Waraqua. Waraqua was, "an old man who had lost his eyesight," ^(Bukhari 6982) but he was also someone who had developed an interest in Christianity. When he heard Muhammad's story, he told him not to worry, saying that he'd read of people visited by angels in the Bible and this was probably a visitation by the angel Gabriel.

Muhammad accepted this explanation but he remained mentally disturbed and still harboured thoughts that he was going insane or had been possessed by an evil spirit. In fact, from this point onwards he became so overcome by depression that he tried to find relief by committing suicide. He said, "Woe is me, poet or possessed. Never shall the Quraysh say this of me! I will go to the top of the mountain and throw myself down that I may kill myself and gain rest." ^(Ibn Ishaq p.106) Bukhari explains, "The prophet became so sad as we have heard that he intended several times to throw himself from the tops of high mountains." ^(Bukhari 9:111)

This went on for some time, but on each occasion, as he was about to launch himself from the mountain, the supernatural being, who he now believed to be Gabriel would block the way and tell him to return home. He said, "I had been thinking of hurling myself down from a mountain crag, but he appeared to me and said, 'Muhammad, I am Gabriel and you are a messenger of God." ^(Al Tabari 1147)

It's interesting that when Muhammad came into contact with this spirit he became suicidal because if we contrast it with the Bible, when the Holy Spirit came upon the Christian believers at Pentecost it paints a very different picture. The Bible says that when the Holy Spirit came on the Christian believers, "A deep sense of awe came over them all, and the apostles performed many miraculous signs and wonders. And all the believers met together in one place and shared everything they had. They sold their property and possessions and shared the money with those in need. They worshipped together at the Temple each day, met in homes for the Lord's supper, and shared their meals with great joy and generosity. All the while praising God and enjoying the goodwill of the people. And each day the Lord added to their fellowship those who were being saved." (Acts 2:42-47) So whereas the coming of the Holy Spirit was marked by awe, joy, generosity, sharing, and goodwill, when this spirit came upon Muhammad in the cave at Hira, that was marked by terror, panic attacks, depression and thoughts of suicide. To quote the Bible, "But I am not surprised! Even Satan disguises himself as an angel of light." (2 Corinthians 11:14)

In the passing of time though, Muhammad settled into the idea that he must be a prophet after all. And with his rich wife's financial backing, he began proclaiming himself to be one. However, the truth is that Muhammad had very little success with his preaching. For the next thirteen years he tried to gather a following but was only really successful with friends and family members. This rejection from the wider Meccan society made Muhammad increasingly frustrated, and he began to show signs of violence in his behaviour. Bukhari reports, "The Prophet entered Mecca and (at that time) there were 360 idols around the Kabah. He started stabbing the idols with a stick he had in his hand and reciting, 'The Truth (Islam) has come and Falsehood has vanished." (Bukhari 3:43:658)

Attacking their idols didn't win the Meccans over. It just made them more upset. So Muhammad then tried yet another

Other Faiths aka Islam

approach. He offered the Meccans a compromise. And the deal was this: If they would finally just agree to pay him some attention and regard him as a prophet, then he would agree to recognise some of their pagan idols in addition to his own Allah, and he would incorporate these other gods into Islam. To solidify this deal, he called down new revelations from Allah who apparently offered his approval for the deal. Muhammad said specifically of three other gods, Allat, Al-Uzza and Manat, "these are the exalted intermediaries whose intercession is to be hoped for!" (Quran 53:19-20)

This idea really pleased the Meccans. "When [the pagan] Quraysh heard this, they rejoiced and were happy and delighted at the way in which he spoke of their gods, and they listened to him, while the Muslims, having complete trust in their prophet in respect of the messages he brought from God, did not suspect him of error, illusion or mistake." (Al Tabari pp.108-109) After the Meccans heard their gods were to be allowed as part of Islam, they then prostrated themselves alongside the Muslims to worship all these multiple gods at once. Al Tabari says, "When [Muhammad] came to the prostration, having completed the surah, he prostrated himself and the Muslims did likewise, following their prophet, trusting in the message which he had brought and following his example. Those polytheists of the Quraysh and others who were in the mosque likewise prostrated themselves because of the reference to their gods which they had heard." (Al Tabari pp.108-109)

The peace between Meccans and Muslims didn't last for very long though, and after listening to more of Muhammad's message, the Meccans once more rejected him. Muhammad didn't take the rejection well, and he quickly retracted all those verses about accepting other gods. He changed his mind and said those verses hadn't really come from Allah at all. He'd actually been tricked. Those messages, he said, had come from Satan. Indeed, those verses have become known as "The Satanic Verses."

Now from whichever angle one views this episode it raises difficult questions for Muslims. Either Muhammad never received any supernatural revelations from Allah at all and was merely making up expedient verses as he went along for influence and personal gain. If that's true, he would be a charlatan and you would need to ask what else he made up for personal gain and inserted into the Quran. The second way of looking at this is that he really did receive those verses from Satan and was unable to tell the difference between Satan's voice and Allah's. If that's true he was a demonically inspired false prophet and you would then need to ask, what else is in the Quran from Satan that he couldn't differentiate? Both options leave his integrity as a prophet in tatters. Because just to be clear, Muhammad openly admitted here to being a mouthpiece for Satan.

Now around this time in 619AD, when Muhammad was 49, he had what's become known as his "year of sorrow." This is the year when his uncle Abu Talib and his wife Khadija both died within a couple of months of each other. This coincided with increasing tensions between the Meccans and Muhammad. Indeed, this was when blood began to flow. When the Meccans criticised a group of Muslims, a Muslim called Sad Bin Abu Waqas had grabbed a camel bone and started beating one of them. This is known as "the first blood to be shed in Islam." (Ibn Ishaq p.118)

The Meccans went to Abu Talib on his deathbed to plead with him to ask Muhammad to leave them alone. They were getting tired of this violence and disruption. A public official said, "You know the trouble that exists between us and your nephew, so call him and let us make an agreement that he will leave us alone and we will leave him alone." (Ibn Ishaq 278) However, even though the Meccans held out this olive branch of peaceful co-existence, Muhammad rejected it and instead chose to keep escalating the violence. The deaths of his closest family members and the constant rejection of his own people seemed to stir up a depressive, nihilistic rage in Muhammad that just couldn't be reasoned with.

Eventually, the situation became untenable. The Meccans decided that Muhammad had to be captured and executed in a bid to end these troubles. In 622AD then, when he was 52 years old, Muhammad was forced to flee Mecca for his life.

He fled to Medina, a town about 450km to the North, and one that had a large Jewish and Christian population. When he arrived there, much like he'd done in Mecca, he initially tried to convert the local population through his preaching. He told the Jews and Christians that he was another prophet in the lineage of their Abraham, Moses and Jesus. He said that his revelation had come through the Angel Gabriel. And that his god, Allah, was the same God as their own.

Much like events in Mecca however, he was rejected by the Jews and Christians. And when you look at his message, it's really no surprise. Firstly, historians note that Muhammad didn't actually introduce any new moral ideas on top of what already existed in the Bible. There was no inspiration in his teaching. When you read the gospels and hear of Jesus' teaching, you are struck by how revolutionary his words were. Jesus said things nobody had ever heard before. He talked about loving enemies, how leaders should wash the feet of servants, and he fundamentally changed the way that people were to relate to God. The Bible often reports that after Jesus had spoken, the crowds were filled with awe because they'd never heard anything like this before. However scholars note that there isn't one single original moral idea in the Quran. Any moral idea you can find in the Quran already existed in the Bible and was borrowed. And even then, because Muhammad was illiterate and had quite a poor grasp of the Bible, whenever he tried to borrow from it, it would often be garbled and confused. For example, Muhammad thought Christians worshipped Mary as the third part of the trinity. (Quran 5:116) Muhammad thought that Mary was the sister of Aaron, even though Aaron was born about 2000 years before Mary. (Quran 19:28) Muhammad thought that Moses spoke to Samaritans, even though Samaritans didn't exist for another 725 years after Moses. (Quran 20:85-88,95) He also confused the life of Saul and Gideon. (Quran 2:249) When you read the Quran, you also get an unmistakeable sense that it's essentially illiterate people trying to ape the Bible's eloquence and style, but not really achieving having the capacity to achieve it. In truth, the text can appear quite nonsensical at times. Basically then, Muhammad himself came across as incompetent in his preaching and Jews and Christians saw these errors and rejected him.

The only original thing that Muhammad actually said to the people of Medina was that he was Allah's prophet and that everyone should do what he says. Hardly a compelling argument. However, so insistent was Muhammad upon it that the idea is repeated 20 times in the Quran and it's also in the Shahada, the Islamic statement of faith, which says, "There is no God but Allah and Muhammad is his messenger." That's the only new message Muhammad brought. So when the Jews and Christians heard his garbled, confused, error-strewn message, they dismissed him.

This pretty much ended Muhammad's attempts to convince people through preaching. From that point onwards he became nothing less than a warlord. Rejected by all, he turned to violence. And he was driven by revenge. Revenge against those who had rejected him. Namely, the Meccans, Jews and Christians.

To enact his revenge, he gathered a group of people and declared they would start waging jihad—a "holy war," as he called it—on all those who had rejected him. They would start by terrorising Meccan caravans as they passed through the area and he promised his followers that if they followed him on this jihad, they would be able to loot these caravans and keep a portion of the bounty they found. He said, "The person who participates in jihad in Allah's cause…will be recompensed by Allah either with a reward, or booty (if he survives) or will be admitted to Paradise (if he is killed in the battle as a martyr." (Bukhari 1:35)

If that wasn't enough to entice the recruits, he promised that as they conquered surrounding towns and villages, they would be able to rape the women too. As he had a habit of doing, he called down expedient revelations from Allah to support his plans. The hadith says, "The Apostle of Allah sent a military expedition to Awtas on the occasion of the battle of Hunain. They met their enemy and fought with them. They defeated them and took them captives. Some of the companions of the Apostle of Allah were reluctant to have intercourse with the female captives in the presence of their husbands who were unbelievers. So Allah, the exalted, sent down the Quranic verse: 'And all married women are forbidden unto you except those captives whom your right hands possess." (Sura 4:24, Abu Dawud 2150. Also Muslim 3433) So conveniently for Muhammad and his followers, Allah suddenly permitted rape of captive women in that exact moment.

Muhammad told volunteers that if they died in jihad for Islam, they would be guaranteed a life of ease in heaven and would be able to copulate with virgin women day and night. Muhammad said, "The humblest of the People of Paradise shall have eighty thousand servants and seventy-two wives." (Sunan al-Tirmidhi 4:21:2687)

For the remaining nine years of his life, Muhammad and his growing band of terrorists waged 95 wars on the surrounding region.[5] That's an average of over 10 wars per year. And the violence got more sadistic as he got older. During those remaining years, he specifically ordered terrorism, beheadings, crucifixions, amputations, torture, child enslavement, rape and more.[6]

On one occasion the hadith reports of some unfortunate souls, "They were caught and brought to Muhammad. He commanded about them, and thus their hands and feet were cut off and their eyes were gouged and then they were thrown into the sun, until they died." (Sahih Muslim 4131) Indeed, his capacity for sadistic torture began to know no bounds. He caught a Jewish tribe called the Banu Qurayza and Ibn Ishaq says, "Then the apostle went out to the market of Medina (which is still its market today) and dug trenches in it. Then he sent for the Banu Qurayza tribe and struck off their heads in those trenches as they were brought out to him in batches…there were 600 or 700 in all though some put the figure as high as 800 or 900." (Ibn Ishaq 464) So in genocidal fury, Muhammad beheaded anywhere up to 900 people in a single day. In 622AD, he also ordered the killing of an elderly woman called Umm Qirfa, "by putting a rope into her two legs and to two camels and driving them until they separated her in two." (Ibn Ishaq) After ripping her in two like this, her severed head was paraded through the streets of Medina.

Muhammad gorged himself on the lusts of his flesh as well. Around this time, when he was 53 years old, he married a six year old girl called Aisha. Bukhari says, "The Prophet married her when she was six-years-old and he consummated his marriage when she was nine-years-old." (Bukhari 7:62:64&65,88) The hadith explicitly reports how he would fondle her in the bath. Aisha said, "The Prophet and I used to take a bath from a single pot…and used to fondle me." (Bukhari 6:298) It also says, "The Prophet used to kiss her and suck her tongue when he was fasting." (Dawud 2386) He encouraged his followers to do the same thing with children. When one of his followers married a woman of similar age to himself he said, "Why didn't you marry a young girl so that you could sport with her and she sport with you, or you could amuse with her and she could amuse with you?" (Muslim 8:3460) Of course, Muhammad continued to call down convenient revelations from Allah to permit him to do whatever he wanted. Aisha actually called him out on his habit of doing this wryly telling him, "I feel that your Lord hastens in fulfilling your desires and wishes." (Bukhari 60:311) Muhammad actually had 11 wives at the same time during this period. Bukhari says, "The Prophet used to visit all his wives in a round, during the day and night and they were eleven in number." (Bukhari 5:268) It also says his clothes became so constantly soiled with semen that he would regularly go to Mosque covered in it. (Bukhari 4:98)

Muhammad owned over 40 slaves in his lifetime. "Muhammad had many male and female slaves. He used to buy and sell them, but he purchased more slaves than he sold. He once sold one black slave for two. His purchase of slaves were more than he sold." (Zad Al-Ma'ad p.160) "Muhammad had a number of black slaves. One of them was named Mahran. Muhammad forced him to do more labour than the average man. Whenever Muhammad went on a trip and he, or his people got tired of carrying their stuff, he made Mahran carry it. Mahran said, "Even if I were carrying the load of 6 or 7 donkeys while we were on a journey, anyone who felt weak would throw his clothes or his shield or sword on me so I would carry that heavy load." (Zad Al-Ma'ad, Tabari & Jawziyya)

Basically, Muhammad's stated goal in the Medina years was nothing less than to conquer, torture, kill and enslave. And again, this was especially true of the groups that had rejected him—the Meccans, the Jews and the Christians. Ultimately though, he wanted the whole world to come under the rule of Islam. Quran 9:33 says Islam is to become "dominant over all other religions." Muhammad said, "Verily Allah has shown me the eastern and western part of the earth, and I saw the authority of my nation dominate all that I saw." (Muslim 2889)

As they set about their task, they were to offer captives just three options. They could either convert to Islam, be subjugated and agree to live as second class citizens, or die. Muhammad said, "Fight those who believe not in Allah nor the Last Day, nor hold that forbidden which hath been forbidden by Allah and His Messenger, nor acknowledge the religion of Truth, (even if they are) of the People of the Book (Jews and Christians), until they pay the Jizya (punitive tax) with willing submission, and feel themselves subdued." (Quran 9:29)

There are in fact 109 violent verses in the Quran that exhort the Muslims to fight unbelievers in that way. In fact the Quran has a kind of split personality. It has some peaceful verses from the Meccan years when Muhammad was still trying to be taken seriously as a prophet in the lineage of Moses and Jesus. But then the Quran has all these violent verses from the Medina years when he'd given up on peace and was waging jihad.

With that mind, we should know that Islam works on a principle of abrogation, meaning all the early peaceful verses have been rendered null and void by the later violent Medina verses. The bottom line is that Islam then is essentially about conquering, killing and dominating the world. Here's a few more verses for clarification: "And fight them until there is no more Fitnah (unbelief in Allah) and the religion will be for Allah alone." (Quran 8:38-39) Also, "The last day will not come about until Muslims fight the Jews, when the Jew will hide behind stones and trees. The stones and trees will say O Muslims, o servant of Allah, there is a Jew behind me, come and kill him." (Bukhari 4:52:177) Also, "But when the forbidden months are past, then fight and slay the pagans wherever you find them, and seize them, beleaguer them, and lie in wait for them in every stratagem of war." (Quran 9:5) "Every stratagem of war" includes deception by the way. According to Islamic teaching, through a practice called "taqiya," Muslims are allowed to lie, deceive and do anything sinful if it furthers the cause of Islam. Therefore, Muslims are allowed to practice deceit, to lie, to make treaties they don't intend to keep to catch their enemies off guard, and basically do anything they want. That means Muslims are inherently untrustworthy when they are trying to further their cause.

And this is how Islam has spread through the world. Not through the strength of Muhammad's teaching which has always been weak and easily rejected, but rather through deception, threats and violence. Indeed, if anyone should try to leave Islam, Muhammad said to kill them. "The Prophet said, if somebody (a Muslim) discards his religion, kill him." (Bukhari 4:52:260) That's the origin of so-called honour killings. And it's why so few people dare to question or leave it. Islam perpetuates itself and sustains itself through intimidation, fear, violence and deceit. It's their modus operandi. And that's because in summary, as we have seen, Muhammad himself was not a prophet from God. He was an illiterate, depressive, demonically possessed, suicidal, paedophile warlord, who commanded slavery, torture, crucifixions, child enslavement, rape, deception and murder. That is who Muhammad was. That is the nature of the religion he founded. And that's why it's incredibly dangerous for the Woke to injudiciously welcome them into the West in their millions. People who have been infected with this ideology soon begin acting like their founder. We have seen it in the West already, and we will continue to see it unless it's tackled head on. If there's not a course correction, and soon, there are going to be some very difficult days ahead.

21
THE WEST

As the previous chapters have highlighted, when talking about Western culture, it's impossible to do that without referencing Christianity—the belief system that gave us our moral foundations and best ideas—and likewise when talking about other cultures it's likewise impossible to do without referencing the religions that formed them. Therefore, when I say that according to this matrix, the Woke believe Western Culture is something to be reviled and pulled down, while every other culture is to be celebrated and raised up, we are still talking around the same area.

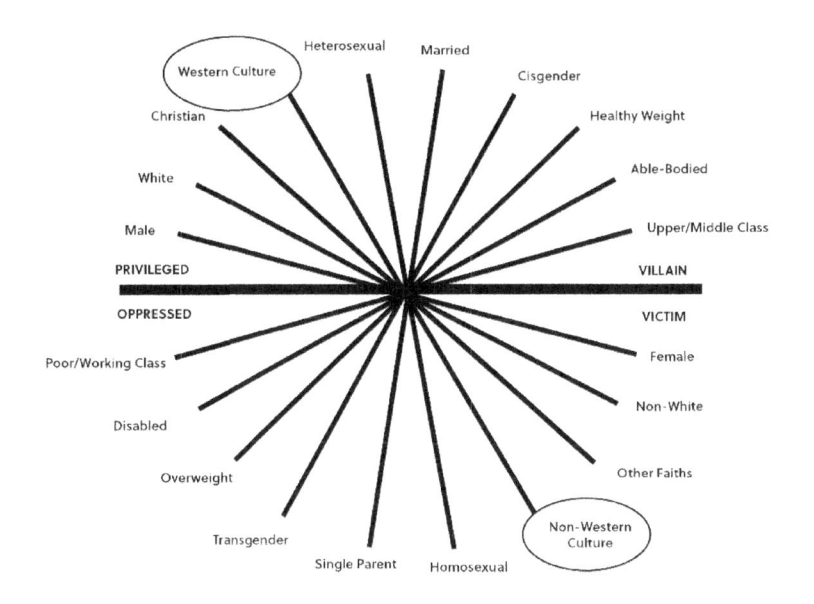

Western Achievements

First, let me explain why it's ridiculous to attempt to tear down the West. As the part of the world that most enthusiastically embraced the teachings of Jesus Christ, it's the place where all the benefits of Christianity that we explored a couple of chapters back first took hold. The West is the place where infanticide was first ended, and human sacrifice, child abandonment, paedophilia, slavery, and killing for entertainment. It was the part of the world that first established free education for all including the blind and deaf, hospitals, nursing, charity. It's the birthplace of the Magna Carta, democracy, ideas of individual liberty, rule of law, trial by jury, and freedom of speech. These are all ideas that we exported to the rest of the world and that consequently made the whole place a nicer environment for everyone.

Earlier in the "What Men Do" chapter I listed some of the inventions that had come from men—bicycles, automobiles, trains, planes, usable electricity, light bulbs, telephones, televisions, vacuum cleaners, computers, the internet, smartphones, the decimal monetary system, flushing toilets, the camera, the hypodermic syringe, penicillin, microwaves, radar, pneumatic tyres, tarmac roads, refrigeration, gasoline, and many of its subsidiary products etc. What I should also mention is that all of these men came from the West. Now that's not to say they couldn't have come from other parts of the world. It's merely to point out that they, in fact, came from the West. Therefore, we can confidently say that Western society has contributed a great deal of technology to the world that has made our lives easier. Indeed, the Industrial Revolution that sparked all this innovation began in Great Britain.

The West has given the world much of humanity's highest cultural achievements. In music, it's the part of the world that gave us Mozart, Beethoven and Bach. In art, it gave us the likes of da Vinci, Michaelangelo, and van Gogh. In literature, it gave us Shakespeare, Dickens and Dumas. The West is home to some of the greatest architectural wonders of the world such as Barcelona's Sagrada Familia, Florence's Cathedral of Santa Maria del Fiore, and Paris' Palace of Versailles.

So successful was the West in becoming a place of beauty, freedom and prosperity, that it has long caused people from other parts of the world to dream of migrating there. To many growing up in the likes of the Middle East, Africa or South East Asia, it was a place of dreams that stirred their hearts. To gain a visa for these countries was akin to winning a golden ticket. And so, as you would expect, world immigration has tended to flow very consistently towards the West. As I have often said, there are no hoards of Swedes desperate to move to Algeria; there are no swathes of Canadians trying to start new lives in Venezuela; there are no crowds of New Zealanders trying to make their way into China. Migration flows in the opposite direction. Why? Because the West has proven to be one of the most attractive places to live in the history of the world.

I feel slightly uncomfortable to be singing the praises of the West like this—it's not a natural thing for us to blow our own trumpet—but it appears that we do need to be reminded. I say this because, due to the influence of Intersectionality Theory, the Woke are currently trying to teach people in the West to **hate** their own culture. This is especially prevalent in schools and universities which appear to have been institutionally captured by the left-wing establishment. They tell their students that the West is inherently evil, racist and corrupt and that no good thing has ever come from it. In their attempts to tear the West down, teachers and lecturers do nothing but denigrate our history, our heroes, and our achievements.

For example, Sir Winston Churchill has long been revered as the man who confronted the evils of Nazi ideology when nobody else would, and who inspired his country to persevere through the dark days of World War II. When the Allies finally defeated Hitler's regime in 1945, Churchill was rightly lauded as being one of the key figures who saved our civilisation. It's shocking to realise then that in educational establishments today, lecturers are teaching children that Churchill was nothing more than a racist warmongering villain. Indeed, such has the vitriol been towards him in recent years that his statue outside the Houses of Parliament has been attacked and graffitied. At one point, it was even boarded up to protect it from harm. Similar things have happened across the West. For example, in 2021, a statue of Thomas Jefferson that had stood in New York City Hall, and that had been there for 187 years, was removed after leftist academics painted him as nothing more than an evil racist.

Constantly being told that your country and civilisation is inherently evil and that nothing, or no one good has ever come of it is having a demoralising effect on the youngest generations. In 1998 , 70% of Americans described patriotism as being very important to them. Today, only 38% do. The younger generations are especially unpatriotic as only 23% of Americans under 30 described patriotism as being very important.[1] Americans are losing love for their country. Indeed, many are becoming openly hateful and ashamed of it. Remember I mentioned Don Crawford encountering a Woke American citizen in 2022 who apparently told him, "I hate Christianity as much as I hate America." I said I would later explain why Americans are beginning to hate America. Well, it's because of this relentless propaganda from the Woke establishment that is particularly keen on poisoning the minds of the young. In a 2021 piece for Newsweek titled, "Why Millennials and Gen Z Aren't Proud To Be American" one college-aged student said, "Learning real American history has made me ashamed to be an American. I've long since detested my heritage, but I have come to despise the country I find myself stuck in. How can anyone learn about this country and feel proud? It confuses and sickens me."[2]

Sentiments like these are growing, and it's why I felt it necessary to trumpet some of the West's historical achievements because the truth is, for all our inevitable human mistakes and problems—and let's not sugarcoat it, there have been many—there is still so much to be proud of. While this student believes he has been taught "real American history," in fact he has been taught Woke propaganda that has left him demoralised and confused. As one put it, kids today are not being taught real history, warts and wall as they assume…they're just being taught warts. That is, they're being taught to see only the worst parts of their history and nothing of the best.

Steven Smith, author of "Reclaiming Patriotism in an Age of Extremes" agrees says, "If students are taught from an early age that America is a country founded on genocide and created to perpetuate slavery—and this has become the ideology of much secondary and higher education—then patriotism will seem nothing more than an expression of bigotry and moral blindness…Students today learn copiously about our national failings—perhaps a corrective to the older triumphalist picture of American history—but not enough about our ideals and aspirations…The names of our national heroes have been erased from schools and public buildings and their statues have been removed. Patriotism requires that we have something to look up to and the current school curricula have become a cure worse than the disease."[2] There is a concerted effort within the left-wing educational establishment to teach students *only* about failings, and nothing about ideals, aspirations or achievements.

Ophelie Jacobson, a conservative student studying at the University of Florida says, "Young people are developing these anti-American sentiments in the classroom. I have spoken to dozens of college students both on and off camera and when I ask them where they develop their ideas, they say college…Disdain for America is only growing stronger. It seems like every day, we are seeing more examples of people who will go to great lengths to show just how ashamed they are to be American…these students don't understand how privileged they are." Tearing down the most successful civilisation in history—and by that I don't just mean America but also the wider West—isn't a good thing to do.

Feeling The Squeeze

This combination of an attractive Western civilisation and a Woke populace who are ashamed of it and blind to its merits, is creating a dangerous situation.

On 23rd November, 2023, a 49-year-old Algerian man who had emigrated to Ireland, armed with a knife, began attacking young children outside a primary school in Dublin. He critically injured three boys and girls between the ages of five and six-years-old, as well as a care assistant in her 30s who tried to intervene to save the children.[3] Far from being an isolated incident, this was merely the latest in a long string of terrorist events in the West involving men from the Islamic world. Whether it be…and take a deep breath before reading this…the twin towers attack in New York (2001), the Madrid bombings (2004), the London bus bombings (2005), the Glasgow airport attack (2007), the Toulouse and Montauban shootings (2012), the Boston marathon bombings (2013), the Lee Rigby murder (2013), the Paris La Défense attack (2013), the Australian Endeavour Hill stabbings (2014), the Canadian Parliament Hill shootings (2014), the New York subway attack (2014), the French Tours police station stabbing (2014), the Charlie Hebdo attacks (2015), Nice stabbing (2015), Copenhagen shootings (2015), Curtis Culwell shootings (2015), Saint-Quentin beheading (2015), Chattanooga shootings (2015), Thalys train attack (2015), Parramatta shooting (2015), Paris attacks (2015), San Bernadino attack (2015), Paris police station attack (2016), Marseille attack (2016), Brussels bombings (2016), Orlando nightclub shootings (2016), Magnanville stabbings (2016), Bastille Day attacks (2016), Wurzberg attacks (2016), Ansbach attacks (2016), Rouen attacks (2016), New York and New Jersey bombings (2016), Ohio State University attacks (2016), Berlin truck attack (2016), Westminster Bridge attacks (2017), Stockholm truck attack (2017), Champs-Elysees attacks (2017), Manchester Arena bombings (2017), London Bridge attack (2017), Notre Dame attack (2017), Barcelona attack (2018), Turku, Finland attack (2017), Parsons Green attack (2017), New York City truck attack (2017), Carcassonne attack (2018), Paris knife attack (2018), Liege attack (2018), Amsterdam stabbings (2018), Melbourne stabbings (2018), Lyon bombing (2019), London Bridge stabbing (2019), Samuel Paty murder (2020), Vienna attack (2020), Auckland attack (2021), Oslo shooting (2022), Cardiff plot (2022), Chateau-Thierry stabbing (2022), Arras school stabbing (2022), the Brussels shooting of 2023, or the Eiffel Tower Attack (2023) these are just some of the ways in which innocent civilians on Western streets have been continually butchered by Islamic men.

Now it's perfectly natural that when you're the subject of sustained attacks over more than two decades from one particular ideology, you want to question that ideology. And when you discover what we now know about the life of Muhammad and the things he taught his followers—that their aim is to subdue and dominate the world using violence and oppression—it's perfectly natural to feel wary that so many with this ideology have imported themselves into your society. These feelings of discomfort are only compounded when the Islamic migrants show no desire to assimilate into Western culture, or to adopt our values, but instead continually seek to impose themselves upon their hosts. Because alongside these regular stories of Islamic terrorism, we have seen mosques being built in our communities, meat on our shelves being quietly switched to halal to appease them, our traditions being cancelled or watered down so as not to offend them, movies being cancelled in response to Islamic protests, and school teachers being intimidated and silenced. Whenever anyone has sought to raise concerns about all this, the Woke establishment have reacted angrily, trying to suppress those voices by calling them racist, bigoted and "Islamophobic." As a minority religion, they believe it must only ever be celebrated.

For a long time then, citizens of the West have felt increasingly squeezed out of their own societies—aliens in their own land—and powerless beneath the rule of governments who demonise them for trying to speak up with legitimate concerns. They have been patient with it all, and if the truth be told, they have also perhaps chosen the line of least resistance, preferring to stay quiet than do anything which may land them in trouble. But the patience, I sense is beginning to run out. For many years, there has been a growing concern about the number of illegal migrants making their way into Europe from the Middle East and North Africa. In 1992, the net migration into the UK was 49,000. By 2023, the net migration has we saw had risen to 745,000.[4] These huge numbers are simply unsustainable and it's meant the infrastructure and economy of the country has started to creak. While the British tax payer has been asked to fund free housing, hotels and food for the migrants at a cost of around £3.6 billion per year (£6million per day), thousands of British citizens themselves are being denied council housing, are now struggling to get a GP appointment, a dentist appointment, and a school place.[5] During a cold snap in December 2023, a story made the news of a man who had died in his car in sub-zero temperatures, while at the same time, an illegal immigrant was making a mockery of the system while living in a tax-payer funded hotel room while making thousands of pounds of the black market. The British people see the unfairness in this and their attitudes are hardening. In the United States, there is a similar situation where illegal immigration is costing $1,156 per taxpayer.[6] The people are beginning to feel impoverished. It's just unaffordable for a finite population of taxpayers to fund an extra burden of this size.

Now history tells us that when people begin to feel the squeeze economically like this, civil war or revolution isn't too far away. That's the worrying thing. Juvenal said that as long as the Roman people had "bread and circuses," they would be appeased. When there was no more bread, the discontent would arise. The French Revolution began when the peasants no longer had any bread too, infamously leading the royalty, who had lost touch and had no understanding of how the people felt to say, "let them eat cake" instead. I have touched upon the economic cost of Woke ideology briefly at various points in this book. It's starting to reach a point where the ordinary person is growing restless.

The sense of unfairness is growing too. Around 2013, it came to light that people primarily of Pakistani ethnicity were grooming and sexually abusing young girls in the UK. It was later discovered that although it was well-known, the authorities were not intervening lest they be accused of racism. In 2020, eleven migrant men hailing from Kuwait, Egypt, Libya and Iran raped a 15-year-old German girl in a park in Hamburg. Two were acquitted while eight of the remaining nine were found guilty, but not sent to jail. They were let off because a Woke psychiatrist claimed that as a victim of "migration experiences and socio-cultural homelessness" they were merely "releasing frustration and anger."[7] They're victims, you see! Carte blanche! Meanwhile the indigenous people who are seeing their sons and daughters being abused like this are becoming incensed. People are asking why the average Westerner should work hard to pay taxes, only for those taxes to be spent on people who hate us, our customs, our traditions, our values, who murder us in our own streets, rape our children, and who openly call for our extermination and subjugation? Why should they be given free housing when our own citizens are denied it and left to die in cars? And why should all our traditions and celebrations established by our ancestors be eradicated to appease them? They ask why they should we be squeezed out of their own country? And in response, the politicians, paralysed by Woke ideology, ignore them and demonise them for even asking the questions.

The Turning Point

When Islamic Hamas terrorists attacked Israel in November of 2023, indiscriminately raping, torturing and murdering 1400 innocent people in cold blood, it seemed to me there was a turning point. Westerners across Europe, North America, Australia and New Zealand saw millions of Hamas supporters flooding out into their city streets in celebration of the terror and in that moment, there was a realisation of just how many with this ideology had been let in, and just how murderous their intentions were. "The barbarians are not at the gates…they're already inside," was a phrase I heard repeatedly.

Fears were further raised on Remembrance Weekend 2023. Every year around November 11th, the British people observe a moment of silence and reflection to remember their ancestors—specifically those who fought and died in World Wars I and II, and indeed any who have fought since to protect our country and keep it safe. It's a time of sombre importance to the nation who wish to pay their respects to the fallen, and the most meaningful ceremonies take place in London around a monument called The Cenotaph. However, on that weekend, rather than respecting the tradition of their host country, thousands of Muslims and pro-Hamas sympathisers took to the streets of London to march through the town, yell about killing Jews, and waving slogans about genocide. It is moments like these that showed the British people more vividly than ever that these people are not in the UK to assimilate and they share no sense of common heritage with us.

From what I can gather from online opinion, there is a resolve that if the West is to be saved, things can't go on like this for much longer. If the politicians don't start paying heed, I really believe there will be a civil conflict. Other countries seem to be waking up to the problems of Woke rule and realigning politically right now. In 2023,

Argentina elected their first right-wing politician in generations—Javier Milei. A couple of weeks later, the Netherlands did the same with Gert Wilders. These elections seem like a cry for change. The British people who had already tried to make their voice heard through Brexit but who have been ignored by a government who then let in 745,000 are now feeling betrayed.

There's a growing anger and the pressure is building. When the Algerian man attacked those Irish children, a group of citizens ran onto the streets of Dublin waving Irish flags and placards with the phrase "Irish Lives Matter." The slogan expressed a fatigue with always having to accept the murder of their people with no real consequences, and always feeling like their own wishes are being set aside to appease illegal migrants who hate them. After the riots, the response of the Irish Prime Minister, Leo Varadkar, was tone-deaf to their concerns. Rather than condemning the Algerian terrorist for trying to kill children, he was only interested with condemning those who had protested it—merely confirming their suspicions that the Woke establishment will always put other cultures before their own. Other cultures they will always raise up. Their own, they will always tear down. Intersectional Theory has conditioned them to do nothing else.

Again, if world leaders continue in this vein, ignoring the concerns of their own people while prioritising illegal immigrants, and if this continues to lead to growing economic hardship, and the feeling Westerners are being squeezed out of their own countries; denied their own birthright; the land of their ancestors; the place they love; with all its traditions and cultural expressions; and if they are denied the chance to hand it to their children, instead being subjugated to appease the concerns of people who openly hate them, I am almost sure there will eventually be a terrible conflict

22
OBESITY

Finally, let's quickly talk about obesity. I wasn't going to because it seems so obvious, but perhaps it is worth mentioning. According to the Woke, people who are overweight are a marginalised segment of society who are looked down upon for their appearance, and therefore, according to their worldview, they are to be celebrated and raised up. Indeed, the more overweight a person is, the more celebrated they should be. As per usual, in an attempt to create a sense of equality, people who are of a healthy weight are also to be pulled down.

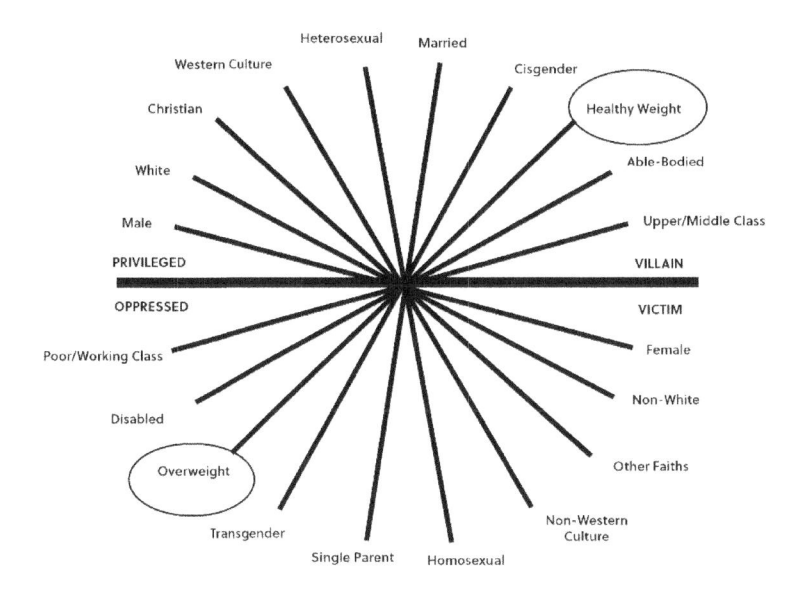

The ways in which obesity is championed are many. Firstly, the woke have sought to normalise it and have encouraged terms such as "plus size" or "fat pride." Obese women have been rebranded as "big beautiful women," while obese models have started to be employed by fashion brands and placed on magazine covers. Some of these models can be genuinely clinically obese, weighing up to around 300lbs (21st.) as was the case of Tess Holliday. Such women are taught that as part of a "body positivity" movement to always be bold and unapologetic about their size. Meanwhile, those who attempt to promote a healthier weight are decried as "fat-shamers" or "body-shamers."

In the Spring of 2015 for example, an advert started appearing on the London Underground asking commuters whether they were "beach body ready." The ad was designed to promote a Protein World slimming product and showed a picture of a thin woman in a bikini. This caused outrage amongst the Woke who said it was "fat shaming" and toxic to tell women that it's better to be thin, and in response, Navabi Fashion made a poster with three clinically obese models saying, "*we're* beach body ready." The message was that obesity is not only normal, but something to take pride in and flaunt. Similarly when the charity, Cancer Research, launched a public health campaign to highlight the links between obesity and cancer, the overweight comedian Sofie Hagen accused them through a series of expletive-laden tweets of "shaming fat people." So determined are the Woke to celebrate obesity and to shut down any messages to the contrary, that some have suggested that when health officials voice their legitimate concerns, it should be treated as a hate crime.

The Problem With Obesity

Again, this one is so obvious that it perhaps doesn't need to be said. While nobody should be bullied for their weight, and while it must be recognised that medications, mental health problems, social deprivation, and genetics all play a role in our ability to control it, and that healthy bodies come in a range of shapes and sizes, if there's one thing we categorically know to be true, it's that true obesity is unhealthy. Cancer Research were correct in asserting that obesity raises the risk. Indeed, according to the Centers for Disease Control and Prevention (CDC) it significantly raises the risk of getting 13 types of cancer.[1] According to the National Institutes of Health, about 4-8% of all cancers are directly attributed to obesity and excess body fat increases the risk of cancer specific mortality by 17%.[2] Obesity also greatly increases the risk of high blood pressure, fatty liver disease, high cholesterol, type 2 diabetes, coronary heart disease, stroke, gallbladder disease, osteoarthritis, sleep apnoea and breathing problems, general body pain, and mental illness. A 2018 study measured the metabolic health of more than 17,000 respondents and discovered that overweight people who exercise regularly and consider themselves "fat but fit" still had a 28% increased risk of heart disease.[3] According to a study by the American Society for Metabolic and Bariatric Surgery, "morbidly obese men weighing an average of 316lbs (143 kgs) between the ages of 35 to 44 had a mortality rate 6 times higher than their lean peers. The rate jumped to 12 times greater for men aged 25 to 34."[4] They added, "obesity accounts for 300,000 deaths per year and severe obesity is associated with a 50 to 60 percent increased risk of death when compared to people who have lower BMIs."[4] In other words, obesity is always dangerous. It will reduce anyone's quality of life and certainly cause early death.

It's especially irresponsible for the Woke to be celebrating unhealthy weight gain today because the truth is we are already in the grip of an obesity epidemic. 27% of British men and 29% of British women are now considered to be clinically obese, which is a massive increase compared to 1980 when only 6% of men and 9% of women were considered so.[5] This means that weight-related hospital admissions in the UK are rising by as much as 18% year-on-year.[3]

At least some of this rise is directly attributable to the Woke "body positivity" movement. In 2019 for example, a story made the news of a 28-year-old Pennsylvanian woman called Megan Fisher, who was unhappy with her 302lbs size and who was intent on shedding the pounds. Just as she was considering gastric bypass surgery, she discovered the aforementioned 300lbs model, Tess Holliday, and being encouraged by her "body positive" message, "realised she too could be happy and confident in her 302 pound body and didn't need to lose weight."[6] By settling for this Holliday inspired size, Fisher was in reality condemning herself to a lower quality of life, accumulating health problems, and shortening her days.

The Hard Truth

The unavoidable conclusion is that it really is better to be within a healthy weight range. The Woke may have their hearts in the right place by trying to make the obese feel better about themselves but they're going about it the wrong way and ultimately causing more harm than good. And if the obese feel shame for their size, perhaps that's not such a bad thing if it leads to real lifestyle change.

I watched a YouTube video recently by Jubilee, where thin and fat people were prompted to have discussions around varying questions related to weight. Among the questions posed were, "Is being fat or skinny a choice?" and "Does America have an obesity problem?" One of the questions was, "Is fat shaming worse than skinny shaming?"

Some of the participants were quick to take the current Woke line that it's wrong to encourage anyone to lose weight, because that would be "fat shaming." They believe people should only ever be celebrated and encouraged to take pride in their body. However, one distinctly overweight man recalled a moment where a friend asked him point blank, "don't you want to be around for your kids?" The man said, "For me, that worked! He was basically telling me, you need to lose weight to be around for your children. I think that worked. That really encouraged me to go to the gym and start trying to lose weight."[7]

Negative emotions like shame are not necessarily something to run from. Often, when we feel them, it's because they're trying to alert us to something that has gone wrong, and they're prompting us to make a change. Have you ever been driving in your car and a warning light pops up on the dashboard? That warning light is a notice that something in your car has been neglected. Something has gone wrong. Something needs to be changed or renewed. We shouldn't ignore such warning lights in our car but we should deal with them as soon as possible. Well that's a bit like what negative emotions are to human beings. Negative emotions alert us to problems.

For example, if we're going along in life and we suddenly feel a sense of guilt for something we said or did, we shouldn't ignore it. Instead, we should pause and reflect. What caused us to feel guilty? Who did we hurt? To whom do we need to apologise? What relationship needs to be repaired? How do we do better going forward? If we respond to that prompt in the right way and make the changes, we'll never find ourselves in that uncomfortable situation again, we'll become better people, and our lives will improve going forward. Likewise, if we suddenly feel lonely, it prompts us to realise perhaps we've been neglecting our character or friendships and we need to put that right. If we feel bored, it prompts us to realise perhaps we're not making the best use of our time. If therefore, someone feels a negative emotions like shame for their obesity, it likewise shouldn't be ignored. Instead, we should ask, what is causing this uncomfortable feeling? What have I done to feel shame? What poor choices have I been making? What do I need to do so that I don't feel this way again in the future? If we respond to these negative emotions in the right way—eating better and hitting the gym—it ultimately leads to a better future.

I had a period around 2019 where I had stopped working out and was overeating. I especially blame chocolate peanuts. I would eat a whole bag in one sitting and I had no idea the calories in those things! As a result, I was around 10-15kgs over my healthy weight. When I realised this, I immediately felt a bit ashamed of the way I'd let myself go. And that was good for me. It meant I started intermittent fasting and going back to the gym—I gave up the chocolate peanuts too—and after many months of consistent resolve, I was back to a healthy place. I have since made it public that if anyone sees me starting to balloon in that way again, fat shame me! I mean it! At the time I didn't realise how much weight I was gaining. Therefore, if it happens again, tell me, so that I can make the necessary changes to live a healthier life. I want to live well, and while it may be difficult to hear at first, the outcome is always worth it.

As usual then, Intersectionality Theory makes a mess of the situation. When applied to this particular area of life, it only promotes poor health, diminished quality of life, and ultimately early death. And let's be honest, we all know this deep down. For even those who claim loudly to be happy with their obesity still strive to lose it when they can, and are happy when they do.

CONCLUSION

Hopefully this book has demonstrated why Intersectionality Theory is so flawed. I began by saying that the intentions of the Woke are basically good—to want to reach out to the marginalised and oppressed. As Christians, we really are on board with this concept. I can't emphasise that enough. However, the framework being used by the Woke to do this is simply for the bin. It is doing *far* more harm than good. And while I write this conclusion in December of 2023, I honestly believe the full extent of that harm is yet to be revealed.

I want to finish this book by briefly though, by saying that if you have enjoyed it, I intend this to be the second part of a trilogy of books. In "Trench"—the first of the trilogy—we looked at why the world has tilted towards far-left ideology. In "The Woke Inversion" I hope I've here shown why the Intersectional framework being used by the far-left is so destructive. However, for the third and concluding part of this journey, I want to present a positive vision for the future. You see, while I think it has been important to expose the flaws in the world's current ideologies and explain why they're failing, I think it's important as a Christian to not only talk about what we're against, but also what we're *for*. I'm aware that in these past two books there's been a lot of negative talk. I've basically been making the point that we're on the wrong road and going into detail about why that's the case. I want to now show what it might look like to be on the *right* road. Let's have some positive talk. Let's imagine a better future.

Indeed, the final part of this trilogy will be called "Imagine." In John Lennon's song of that name, he asks the world to imagine a world with no religion, no country and no possessions. He says this would make the world a wonderful place to be. Of course, this is also nonsense. But I'd like to put a Christian spin on that basic premise. I want to ask the world to imagine what it would be like if all turned to Jesus and his precepts—not through a song but through a book—and to explain just how that would change it for the better. I'm excited about inviting you to dream along with me in that volume.

In the meantime, my immediate plan is to turn this book into a video series which will be released on YouTube and Rumble in weekly episodes. Make sure to subscribe to The Fuel Project social media accounts to get notified when a new episode is released, and if you'd like to support The Fuel Project financially through this period, you can do so at Patreon, GiveSendGo or PayPal. The details of how to do that are at the end of this book in the "About The Fuel Project" section (after the bibliography).

Thank you for reading. Whether you're a Christian or not, I hope this book has been useful and that you feel equipped with a greater understanding of the times in which we live. Intersectional Theory is not the answer. Jesus is.

God bless
Mark   Fairley

BIBLIOGRAPHY & NOTES

SECTION 1

Chapter 1 – Hatred

1. https://en.wikipedia.org/wiki/Intersectionality
2. https://www.washingtonpost.com/education/2021/06/09/yale-lecturer-talks-about-killing-white-people/
3. https://www.theamericanconservative.com/heteronormativity-smashers-elly-barnes/
4. https://www.dailymail.co.uk/news/article-12230639/Were-coming-children-Topless-activists-drag-queens-spark-outrage-NYC-Pride.html
5. https://www.merriam-webster.com/dictionary/woke

Chapter 2 – The Male Privilege Myth

1. https://www.dailymail.co.uk/sciencetech/article-6564767/Men-face-discrimination-women.html
2. https://en.wikipedia.org/wiki/Sentencing_disparity
3. https://www.penalreform.org/global-prison-trends-2022/prison-populations/#:~:text=Men%20make%20up%20most%20of,Drugs%20and%20Crime%20(UNODC).
4. https://www.theguardian.com/news/datablog/2013/may/07/men-gender-divide-feminism
5. https://www.youtube.com/watch?v=OFpYj0E-yb4
6. https://www.armyandnavyacademy.org/blog/why-so-many-male-students-are-falling-behind-in-school/
7. https://familylawattorneymesaaz.net/divorce-for-men-why-do-women-get-child-custody-more-often/
8. https://www.co-oplegalservices.co.uk/media-centre/articles-jan-apr-2017/divorce-with-kids-who-gets-the-house/

9. https://www.ncbi.nlm.nih.gov/pmc/articles/PMC5992251/#:~:text=In%20the se%20domains%2C%20several%20studies,after%20separation%20(Shor%20et %20al.
10. https://trdsf.com/blogs/news/the-10-most-dangerous-jobs-in-the-world
11. https://www.eviemagazine.com/post/woman-pretended-to-be-a-man-dies-assisted-suicide-realizing-difficult
12. https://www.tiktok.com/@wearemanenough/video/7242347543034793262
13. https://api.army.mil/e2/c/downloads/2022/11/15/62a2d64b/active-component-demographic-report-october-2022.pdf
14. https://www.priorygroup.com/blog/why-are-suicides-so-high-amongst-men

Chapter 3 – The White Privilege Myth

1. https://www.dailymail.co.uk/news/article-11084863/Anger-taxpayer-funded-charity-erects-Hey-Straight-White-Men-Pass-Power-billboards.html
2. https://www.gbnews.com/opinion/white-privilege-is-a-myth-and-a-divisive-and-dangerous-myth-at-that-says-darren-grimes/346045
3. https://www.spectator.co.uk/article/working-class-boys-and-the-myth-of-white-privilege/
4. https://thecritic.co.uk/issues/december-2019/no-need-to-plead-guilty/
5. https://www.spectator.co.uk/article/working-class-boys-and-the-myth-of-white-privilege/

Chapter 4 - Inverting Status

1. https://www.goodreads.com/quotes/522869-i-think-it-s-important-to-have-a-good-hard-failure
2. https://www.theguardian.com/education/2005/jan/11/schools.uk1

Chapter 5 – The Victimhood Olympics

1. https://www.scottishpoetrylibrary.org.uk/poem/sair-finger/
2. https://committees.parliament.uk/work/6967/covid19-employment-support-schemes/news/186552/government-lacks-proof-of-impact-of-97-billion-of-taxpayers-money-spent-on-furlough-and-self-employed-job-support/

Bibliography and Notes

3. https://www.nytimes.com/2021/01/27/movies/harvey-weinstein-settlement.html
4. https://eu.freep.com/story/news/local/michigan/detroit/2017/12/18/stephen-henderson-fired-wdet-free-press/960580001/
5. https://www.dailymail.co.uk/news/article-5833061/Netflix-bans-workers-looking-five-seconds-flirting-crackdown.html

Chapter 6 – The Benefits of Victimhood

1. https://www.dailymail.co.uk/news/article-10124065/Former-Labour-MP-reportedly-fears-discriminated-against-faces-jail.html
2. https://www.dailymail.co.uk/news/article-10004111/NHSs-diversity-tsar-paid-35-000-chief-executive.html
3. https://www.express.co.uk/news/uk/1452228/bbc-job-advert-bans-white-people-bame-ethnic-minorities-uk-media-jobs
4. https://news.sky.com/story/raf-recruiters-were-advised-against-selecting-useless-white-male-pilots-to-hit-diversity-targets-12893684

Chapter 7 – Enfeebled

1. https://www.youtube.com/watch?v=owiWBI--R8E
2. https://www.youtube.com/watch?v=sWbj-2DRLps
3. https://www.youtube.com/watch?v=v8UEkkDDlvE&t=29s
4. https://www.youtube.com/watch?v=mbvH-Q-ZyJ4&t=593s

Chapter 8 – Division

1. https://www.huffingtonpost.co.uk/entry/why-men-are-really-trash_uk_5ae97b12e4b081860d8ca14d
2. https://ifstudies.org/blog/theres-no-huge-gender-gap-in-being-single-among-young-adults
3. https://www.sltrib.com/sponsored/2023/08/01/are-passport-bros-really-problem/
4. https://care.org.uk/news/2022/05/marriage-rate-lowest-on-record
5. https://www.ed.ac.uk/health/research/centres/ccri/first-thursday-seminars-21_22/whiteness-a-problem-for-our-time

6. https://www.insidehighered.com/news/2022/11/09/university-chicago-postpones-course-whiteness
7. https://medium.com/message/whiteness-3ead03700322
8. https://modernismmodernity.org/forums/whiteness-problem
9. https://harvardmagazine.com/2002/09/abolish-the-white-race-html
10. https://blog.pmpress.org/2019/09/16/the-point-is-not-to-interpret-whiteness-but-to-abolish-it/
11. https://www.wired.com/story/mohsin-hamid-the-last-white-man/
12. https://edition.cnn.com/2016/12/26/health/drexel-professor-white-genocide-trnd/index.html
13. https://www.cambridgema.gov/-/media/Files/officeofthemayor/2019/whypeopleofcolorneedspaceswithoutwhitepeople1.pdf
14. https://www.theguardian.com/commentisfree/2017/may/30/white-people-black-women-feminist-festival
15. https://www.dailymail.co.uk/news/article-12804889/BBC-presenter-says-overwhelmingly-white-workplace-affects-mental-health.html

Chapter 9 – Paranoia

1. https://www.aknowbrainer.com/_files/ugd/9e22b0_b435afb90e8b4cae821b969f6464447f.pdf
2. https://www.youtube.com/watch?v=t7nsAMwl1T4 (Billy Connolly - Dwarf on a Bus – Live in London 2010)
3. https://www.bbc.co.uk/news/uk-england-dorset-57611781

Chapter 10 – Uncharitable

1. https://www.youtube.com/watch?v=bmSiKiFNYSY

SECTION 2

Chapter 12 – What Men Do

1. "All Men Are Trash" by Pancho (https://www.youtube.com/watch?v=0xc-neCMspk&t=195s)
2. Why Hollywood secretly HATES women by Baggage Claim https://www.youtube.com/watch?v=kq49SvoLoH8
3. https://www.ranken-energy.com/index.php/products-made-from-petroleum/
4. https://careersmart.org.uk/occupations/equality/which-jobs-do-men-and-women-do-occupational-breakdown-gender
5. https://www.statista.com/statistics/195324/gender-distribution-of-full-time-law-enforcement-employees-in-the-us/
6. https://www.bls.gov/opub/ted/2021/men-accounted-for-about-75-percent-of-workers-in-protective-service-occupations-in-2020.htm
7. https://en.wikipedia.org/wiki/Royal_National_Lifeboat_Institution
8. https://www.stemgraduates.co.uk/women-in-stem?source=google.com
9. Expedite Robinson (2002) https://www.youtube.com/watch?v=3uc2EtMhoKU&list=PLmLJ4za8Ug9pEv5i7tjPqBfWMf-4_I657
10. https://www.brainyquote.com/quotes/camille_paglia_159814
11. This can be seen on YouTube by searching for Men Vs Women Survival. At the time of writing is has been split into several parts.
12. https://www.aei.org/society-and-culture/crucial-importance-stay-home-wives/

Chapter 13 – What Women Do

1. https://www.golfdigest.com/story/reddit-golf-friend-story
2. https://www.dazeddigital.com/life-culture/article/57460/1/straight-men-no-friends-toxic-masculinity-loneliness-u-ok
3. https://careersmart.org.uk/occupations/equality/which-jobs-do-men-and-women-do-occupational-breakdown-gender
4. https://www.aei.org/society-and-culture/crucial-importance-stay-home-wives/

Chapter 14 – Marriage Benefits Adults

1. https://economictimes.indiatimes.com/magazines/panache/being-married-can-be-beneficial-to-men-heres-why/articleshow/97031567.cms
2. https://www.psychologytoday.com/us/blog/best-practices-in-health/202306/how-loneliness-can-impact-our-health-and-lifespan#:~:text=Key%20points,for%20both%20men%20and%20women
3. https://bigthink.com/smart-skills/married-wage-gap/#:~:text=That%20married%20people%20make%20more,to%20be%20greater%20for%20men.
4. https://www.city-journal.org/article/why-marriage-is-good-for-you

Chapter 15 – Marriage Benefits Kids

1. https://www.theguardian.com/business/2022/jul/04/half-of-all-children-in-lone-parent-families-are-in-relative-poverty
2. https://www.fatherhood.org/father-absence-statistic
3. https://fathers.com/the-consequences-of-fatherlessness/
4. https://www.all4kids.org/news/blog/a-fathers-impact-on-child-development/#:~:text=Children%20who%20feel%20a%20closeness,to%20experience%20multiple%20depression%20symptoms.
5. https://www.afathersplace.org/why-it-matters/fathers/
6. https://parentspluskids.com/blog/fatherhood-statistics-trends-and-analysis
7. https://www.all4kids.org/news/blog/a-fathers-impact-on-child-development/
8. Dads help curb violence at Louisiana High School (CBS Evening News) https://www.youtube.com/watch?v=OdPaqt6RY_Q

Chapter 16 – Homosexuality

1. https://www.ons.gov.uk/peoplepopulationandcommunity/culturalidentity/sexuality/bulletins/sexualidentityuk/2017
2. The reason I chose the statistics from 2012 was because I wanted numbers from before the time when the contagion of Intersectionality took effect and started skewing them.
3. https://dictionary.cambridge.org/dictionary/english/normal
4. https://www.merriam-webster.com/dictionary/natural

5. See the earlier references where we saw Woke figures calling to "smash heteronormativity."
6. https://www.9marks.org/article/from-lesbianism-to-complementarianism/
7. https://josephsciambra.com/i-was-the-other-man-an-insiders-look-at-why-gay-marriage-will-never-work/
8. The video containing the original comments can be found in a discussion Jordan Peterson had with Dave Rubin on the latter's YouTube channel. I originally referenced it however in a September 2023 Fuel Project video called "The Trauma Theory." It can be found here: https://youtu.be/1DgmMKMpIvY
9. https://news.vumc.org/2022/02/24/study-finds-lgbq-people-report-higher-rates-of-adverse-childhood-experiences-than-straight-people-worse-mental-health-as-adults/
10. https://pubmed.ncbi.nlm.nih.gov/11501300/
11. https://www.ncbi.nlm.nih.gov/pmc/articles/PMC3535560/
12. https://mhanational.org/issues/lgbtq-communities-and-mental-health
13. https://www.cdc.gov/std/life-stages-populations/stdfact-msm.htm#:~:text=Am%20I%20at%20risk%20for,HIV%20infections%20occur%20among%20MSM.
14. https://www.cdc.gov/hiv/group/gender/men/index.html
15. https://www.cdc.gov/msmhealth/STD.htm
16. https://www.bbc.co.uk/news/health-13295300
17. https://pubmed.ncbi.nlm.nih.gov/9923159/
18. https://news.feinberg.northwestern.edu/2014/09/18/carroll-domestic-violence/
19. https://ncadv.org/blog/posts/domestic-violence-and-the-lgbtq-community
20. https://www.plymouth.gov.uk/sexual-health-2022#:~:text=Sexual%20ill%2Dhealth%20has%20been,%C2%A3280%2C000%20and%20%C2%A3360%2C000.

Chapter 17 – Transgenderism

1. https://www.ons.gov.uk/peoplepopulationandcommunity/culturalidentity/genderidentity/bulletins/genderidentityenglandandwales/census2021
2. https://www.hopkinsguides.com/hopkins/view/Johns_Hopkins_Psychiatry_Guide/787024/all/Delusions?q=Herp
3. https://www.merriam-webster.com/dictionary/psychosis

4. All of these are real life examples.
5. https://www.dailymail.co.uk/news/article-4367098/Man-desperate-healthy-leg-AMPUTATED.html
6. https://www.dailymail.co.uk/news/article-12139475/Parents-rail-against-school-district-book-teaches-kids-transgender.html
7. https://www.theguardian.com/uk-news/2023/jan/31/scottish-ministers-say-they-did-not-know-rapist-isla-bryson-was-put-in-womens-prison
8. https://en.wikipedia.org/wiki/Isla_Bryson_case#:~:text=Bryson%20appeared%20in%20court%20in,Bryson%20in%20court%20that%20year.
9. https://nypost.com/2022/08/05/trans-prisoner-who-impregnated-two-women-is-psychopath/
10. https://www.lifesitenews.com/news/transgender-female-boxer-gives-female-opponent-concussion-breaks-her-eye-so/
11. https://www.espn.com/mma/story/_/id/32186035/transgender-fighter-alana-mclaughlin-submits-celine-provost-mma-debut
12. https://unherd.com/thepost/girls-assaulted-in-gender-neutral-toilets-as-predicted/
13. https://apnews.com/article/loudoun-virginia-lawsuit-transgender-bathroom-sexual-assault-a26168568cc20c2aa6cec9bef50e7c3f
14. https://www.bbc.co.uk/news/health-51676020
15. https://www.scottishdailyexpress.co.uk/news/uk-news/man-sues-nhs-same-day-27318325
16. https://www.dailymail.co.uk/news/article-12113249/Christian-teacher-suspended-misgendering-trans-pupil-banned-teaching.html

Chapter 18 – Contagion

1. https://www.ipsos.com/en-us/news-polls/ipsos-lgbt-pride-2021-global-survey
2. Figures as reported by The Guardian (24th November, 2022) https://www.theguardian.com/society/2022/nov/24/an-explosion-what-is-behind-the-rise-in-girls-questioning-their-gender-identity
3. Triggernometry Podcast with Miriam Grossman. https://www.youtube.com/watch?v=SzyG5Zmm_tY
4. https://www.geldards.com/insights/new-report-reveals-true-scale-of-family-breakdown-in-the-uk/
5. https://www.nicswell.co.uk/health-news/absent-fathers-linked-to-depression-risk-in-girls

Bibliography and Notes

6. https://www.familylaw.co.uk/news_and_comment/CentreSocialJustice08022011-963

Chapter 19 – Christianity

1. https://theweek.com/articles/443225/why-many-liberals-despise-christianity
2. https://www.dailymail.co.uk/news/article-2046959/Police-say-sorry-cafe-owner-threatened-arrest-Bible-DVDs.html
3. https://www.dailymail.co.uk/news/article-2046959/Police-say-sorry-cafe-owner-threatened-arrest-Bible-DVDs.html
4. https://www.standard.co.uk/news/uk/christian-couple-blocked-from-adopting-foster-children-amid-gay-parents-row-a3388456.html#:~:text=Christian%20couple%20blocked%20from%20adopting%20foster%20children%20amid%20'gay%20parents'%20row,-'Concerning%20views'%3A&text=A%20Christian%20couple%20have%20been,a%20%E2%80%9Cmummy%20and%20daddy%E2%80%9D.
5. https://www.bbc.co.uk/news/uk-england-birmingham-49904997
6. https://christianconcern.com/ccpressreleases/christian-nurse-sacked-for-wearing-cross-necklace-wins-legal-case/
7. https://www.dailymail.co.uk/news/article-6040923/Christian-nurse-sacked-giving-patient-Bible-allowed-work.html
8. For example, David McConnel or Ryan Schiavo in 2023.
9. https://medium.com/tryangle-magazine/if-jesus-comes-back-this-guy-will-kill-him-264ddaaf8651
10. https://crawfordmediagroup.net/the-new-anti-american-woke-culture/
11. As quoted in How Christianity Changed The World by Alvin J Schmidt
12. https://www.washingtontimes.com/news/2017/oct/30/religious-people-more-likely-give-charity-study/
13. https://www.businessinsider.com/everyday-phrases-shakespeare-made-up-2016-3?r=US&IR=T
14. https://www.churchtimes.co.uk/articles/2019/27-september/features/features/tom-holland-interview-we-swim-in-christian-waters

Chapter 20 – Other Faiths aka Islam

1. https://www.gov.uk/government/statistics/irregular-migration-to-the-uk-year-ending-june-2023/irregular-migration-to-the-uk-year-ending-june-2023
2. https://www.theguardian.com/uk-news/2023/nov/23/net-migration-to-uk-hit-record-745000-in-2022-revised-figures-show#:~:text=The%20Office%20for%20National%20Statistics,unexpected%20patterns%E2%80%9D%20in%20migrant%20behaviour.
3. https://en.wikipedia.org/wiki/Allah_as_a_lunar_deity
4. https://en.wikipedia.org/wiki/Abdullah_ibn_Abd_al-Muttalib
5. https://themuslimvibe.com/faith-islam/abu-talib-the-uncle-of-prophet-muhammad
6. https://en.wikipedia.org/wiki/List_of_expeditions_of_Muhammad
7. Examples of terrorism are found at Quran 8:60 and Quran 8:12. Examples of beheadings are found at Quran 8:12 and Quran 47:4. Crucifixions are ordered at Quran 5:33 and in Abu Dawud 38:4339. Amputations are at Quran 8:12 and Quran 5:33. Torture is reported by Ibn Ishaq. Child enslavement is evidenced at Bukhari 5:512. Rape is found at Bukhari 7:137. Murder is found at Muslim 4131. Genocide is ordered at Ibn Ishaq 464. There are many other examples of such things.

Chapter 21 – The West

1. https://www.newsweek.com/my-generationgen-z-being-taught-hate-america-we-have-resist-opinion-1791245
2. https://www.newsweek.com/patriotism-gap-millennials-gen-z-baby-boomers-gen-x-1611749
3. https://en.wikipedia.org/wiki/2023_Dublin_riot#:~:text=On%2023%20November%202023%2C%20at,in%20Parnell%20Square%20East%2C%20Dublin.
4. https://twitter.com/GoodwinMJ/status/1727622496411627803
5. https://hansard.parliament.uk/commons/2023-06-27/debates/ABE8419C-FAF8-4D97-A09F-DC765DAD72CF/IllegalMigrationBillEconomicImpactAssessment
6. https://us.iaservices.org.uk/cost-of-illegal-immigration-how-much-does-illegal-immigration-cost-the-us-each-year/
7. https://dailycaller.com/2023/11/28/gang-rape-germany-2020-suspended-sentence/

Chapter 22 – Obesity

1. https://www.cdc.gov/cancer/obesity/index.htm
2. https://www.ncbi.nlm.nih.gov/pmc/articles/PMC9857053/#:~:text=Obesity%20has%20been%20linked%20to,cancers%20are%20attributed%20to%20obesity.
3. https://www.theguardian.com/commentisfree/2018/apr/10/fat-pride-obesity-public-health-warnings-dangerous-weight-levels
4. https://health.howstuffworks.com/diseases-conditions/death-dying/5-causes-of-death-for-people-over-300-pounds.htm
5. https://ukhsa.blog.gov.uk/2021/03/04/patterns-and-trends-in-excess-weight-among-adults-in-england/
6. https://www.dailymail.co.uk/femail/article-7188845/Plus-sized-woman-28-proudly-shows-300LBS-body-bikinis.html
7. https://www.youtube.com/watch?v=Eo0qwArsmpA

ABOUT THE FUEL PROJECT

The Fuel Project was established around 2011 with the sole purpose of informing, inspiring and igniting Christian faith. The aim has always been to do it by engaging with our world in Biblical and creative ways—whether that be through words, video, film, photography, art, music, technology or animation—we want to reach people however we can.

Over the years, we have covered a wide range of subjects. Other topics include freedom, legalism, the church, end-time prophecy, postmodernism, porn and masturbation, anxiety and depression, Biblical happiness, politics and current events. If you have enjoyed this book and would like to explore more about the other titles, please visit our website:

thefuelproject.org

If you would like to purchase any of the books relating to these subjects, they are all available in paperback and e-book format from **Amazon**. You can go to Amazon directly and search for Mark Fairley or The Fuel Project. Alternatively, there are relevant links on The Fuel Project website under the "Store" tab.

If you prefer to consume information by video, almost all the books have been converted into series that are available on **YouTube** and **Rumble**. In general, videos are released on a weekly basis. Our channels can be found at:

youtube.com/thefuelproject
rumble.com/thefuelproject

Please subscribe to the channels and click the notification icon where present to be informed whenever a new video is released. If you would like to download personal copies of any video series, you can also visit:

thefuelproject.org/downloads

Please also consider subscribing to our other social media channels:

X – x.com/thefuelproject

Facebook – facebook.com/thefuelproject

Instagram – instagram.com/thefuelproject

Threads – threads.com/thefuelproject

All the ministry's latest activity can also be found at the "News" section of our website. If you'd like to find out what we've been up to, or would like to know what we're planning for the future, the address to visit is:

thefuelproject.org/news

Finally, The Fuel Project is made possible through financial support, primarily on Patreon. If you would like to contribute to this work, you can do so from as little as $2 a month. The page can be found at:

patreon.com/thefuelproject

Support us on
PATREON
patreon.com/thefuelproject

It's also now possible to support our work on GiveSendGo—a Christian crowdfunding platform committed to the preservation of free speech. The page can be found at:

givesendgo.com/thefuelproject

GiveSendGo

PayPal donations can also be made using the email address, authenticfuel@gmail.com.

PayPal

Alternatively, you can also donate using credit and debit cards by going to our website and clicking the "Donate" button at the top-right corner. As a small ministry which depends on its patrons to survive, all support is greatly appreciated and will help ensure that The Fuel Project can continue to exist, and hopefully even grow in the future.

At the time of writing this book, 189 people have written to say they became a Christian as a direct result of this ministry. However, since most don't communicate their conversions and I only tend to find out in incidental ways, I believe that the real number is possibly much higher. I hope even more that many more thousands will come to Jesus through this ministry in the years ahead.

This book will now be turned into a video series with episodes being released on a weekly basis. If you'd like to follow along with the episodes, make sure to subscribe to the previously mentioned social media links. If you're reading this book more than a few months after this book's release, the project will likely already have been completed and will be available for download.

Thank you for supporting this ministry with your purchase and for reading. I hope the information within has proven helpful for your understanding of the times in which we live.

Mark Fairley
The Fuel Project

Printed in Great Britain
by Amazon